Light Verse
from the
Floating World

Light Verse
from the
Floating World

An Anthology of Premodern Japanese Senryu

Compiled, Translated, and

with an Introduction by

MAKOTO UEDA

Columbia

University

Press

New York

Columbia University Press

Publishers Since 1893

New York   Chichester, West Sussex

Copyright © 1999 Columbia University Press

All rights reserved

Library of Congress Cataloging-in-Publication Data

Light verse from the floating world : an anthology of premodern
  Japanese senryu / compiled, translated, and with an introduction by
  Makoto Ueda.

  p.   cm.

  Includes bibliographical references.

  ISBN 0-231-11550-4 (cloth). — ISBN 0-231-11551-2 (pbk.)

  1. Senryū—Translations into English. I. Ueda, Makoto, 1931–   .

PL782.E3L44   1999

895.6'1070803—dc21   99-20630
                                                          CIP

Casebound editions of Columbia University Press books are printed
on permanent and durable acid-free paper.

Printed in the United States of America

c 10 9 8 7 6 5 4 3 2 1

Columbia University Press wishes to express its appreciation of assistance
given by the Pushkin Fund in the publication of this anthology.

Contents

Preface

       This is a collection of some four hundred humorous and comic poems from premodern Japan written in a seventeen-syllable verse form known as *senryu*. Strictly speaking, it is not quite right to call them senryu, because there was no such usage when they were written. Contemporaries knew them as *maekuzuke* (verse capping), *kyōku* (mad verse), *zareku* (playful verse), and by several other names. Senryu as the name of a poetic genre came into existence in the mid-nineteenth century and became well established only in the twentieth century. Today it is common practice in Japan to apply the term to all poems belonging to the genre, regardless of when they were written, and that is what I have done here, although I have not used the long-vowel marker over the "u." I have not done so because I expect the word senryu to become completely anglicized in the near future, when the verse form will have reached the level of international popularity enjoyed by haiku today.

    Senryu, like haiku, is a short unrhymed verse with the 5–7–5 syllable pattern. Unlike haiku, however, it requires no word implying the season of the year, as it draws less on nature than on human nature. Whereas a haiku poet in general tries to capture a moment of insight into the mysterious workings of the natural world, a writer of senryu keenly studies various aspects of the human condition and reports his findings in a humorous way, the humor sometimes crossing over to the territory of satire. Senryu differs from haiku in its rhetoric, too, since it seldom uses the common haiku technique known as internal comparison. Whereas a haiku often juxtaposes two disparate objects and challenges the reader to make an imaginary connection between them, a typical senryu presents one unique situation and asks the reader to view it in the light of reason or common sense. The reader who does that will usually experience a feeling of superiority, or of incongruity, or of relief, which in turn will lead to laughter. It is not without reason that senryu is often translated as "comic verse" or "satirical poetry."

The collection is divided by topics into ten sections. The opening two sections are by and large satirical, the first aimed at people of the ruling warrior class and the second at civilians engaged in various professions. The next four sections comprise senryu that deal with specific human relationships: between young lovers, between husband and wife, between parent and child, and between family members of different generations. The seventh section features townsmen enjoying themselves in the amusement districts, while the eighth sketches their lives against the background of the four seasons. After ridiculing a number of well-known historical figures in the ninth section, the anthology ends with a group of verses that reveal the writers' general outlook on life. I have added a general introduction and a selected bibliography.

The book is intended for those who do not read Japanese. Readers with a knowledge of Japanese should read senryu in the original language and appreciate its linguistic features that cannot be translated. As listed in the bibliography, a great number of premodern senryu are available in modern editions, many of which come with annotations and indexes. For the purpose of identification, I have provided the original verse in romanized form at the bottom of each page. The letter (or letters) and number that appear in the parentheses following each original verse indicate the source, a system explained in the section headed "Sources." A large majority of the selected verses will be found in Okada Hajime, ed., *Haifū yanagi-daru zenshū*, 12 vols. (Tokyo, 1976–78).

All Japanese names in the book are in the Japanese order, with the surname preceding the given name or *gagō* (pseudonym), except where they appear as authors of books in English. The Japanese in premodern times used the lunar calendar, but I have converted all dates into their equivalents in the Gregorian calendar as accurately as I could.

I have to confess that translating senryu turned out to be a task considerably more challenging than I had expected. More than any other type of Japanese poetry, senryu abounds in colloquialisms and slang words as well as in allusions to popular customs and manners that are long gone. In interpreting individual poems, I am indebted to a number of Japanese scholars whose names are listed in the bibliography. Having grasped the meaning of each poem, I then faced the equally difficult task of transmitting its humor to English. Humor is hard to covey in translation, especially when the original and the target language are as far apart as Japanese and English. I am, therefore, all the more grateful to Mr. J. Michael Edwards, who carefully went over the entire manuscript and made numerous suggestions to make the translations sound more humorous or satirical. I also wish to thank the three anonymous readers provided by Columbia University Press, each of whom offered a number of valuable comments to help improve the manuscript. However, I alone am responsible for all the errors and infelicities that may be found in the book.

m.u.

Light Verse
from the
Floating World

Introduction

The word *senryu* is derived from the name of a person, Karai Senryū (1718–1790), who lived in the downtown district of Edo, a city now known as Tokyo. His real name was Karai Hachiemon, and he made a living as the head official of his ward, a position he had inherited from his father at the age of about thirty-six. Perhaps his work was boring, or perhaps it did not bring him much income. For whatever reason, in 1757 he decided to make a debut as a master of *maekuzuke*, a verse-writing game played by a good many people in Japan at that time. Senryū, which literally means "river willow," was the professional name he adopted on becoming a master. His home was near a river, so probably there was a willow tree too.

Maekuzuke was originally a method of teaching how to link verses, but by Senryū's time it had evolved into a popular poetry contest. In such a contest, the master would first announce the *maeku* (previous verse), usually containing two lines of seven Japanese syllables each.[1] For example, one of the maeku Senryū used in a contest several months after his debut was

just in case it should happen   *moshi ya moshi ya to*
just in case it should happen   *moshi ya moshi ya to*

---

[1] *Premodern Japanese poets made no use of lineation as such. From the earliest times, however, a poem progressed in units of a certain number of syllables (five and seven in most instances), each unit usually ending with a grammatical break. A large majority of translators have seen it fit to render these units as lines in English. I have therefore decided to call them "lines" in this book.*

Anyone who wanted to enter the contest was to add a *tsukeku* (following verse) of 5–7–5 syllables in such a way that the two verses combined would make a good poetic sequence. To use the example cited above, one entrant for the contest submitted the tsukeku,

at the teahouse	*mizuchaya e*
he puffs rings of smoke	*kite wa wa wo fuki*
all day long	*hi wo kurashi (Y 1)*[2]

which seems to picture a shy young man who is secretly in love with a waitress working at the teahouse. The man smokes like a chimney and never leaves, just in case the waitress might notice his persistence and take an interest in him. The same maeku inspired another contestant to contribute the tsukeku,

men all but naked	*fundoshi ni*
and a man with a club	*bōtsuki no iru*
in the hills of Sado	*Sado no yama (Y 1)*

which presents a scene at a gold mine on the island of Sado. The miners are at work wearing nothing but loincloths so that they would have nowhere to hide any ore; still, just in case, there is a guard constantly watching them.

The amateur poets who submitted verses to those contests had to pay a small entry fee. In return, they could win prizes such as cotton fabric, a set of bowls, a tray, and so forth. The winning verses were printed and distributed to various poets' groups that had helped in advertising the contest and collecting entries. The person who screened the submitted verses was the maekuzuke master, known as *tenja* (referee), who had written the maeku.

Karai Senryū, who started as a totally unknown tenja in

---

[2] *The letter (or letters) and the number within parentheses after a premodern senryu indicate the source. For explanation, see the section "Sources."*

1757, eventually became the most influential master of maekuzuke in Japan. It is estimated that he refereed more than 2.3 million verses during his lifetime. Because of his fame, maekuzuke and Senryū became almost synonymous. Later on, when tsukeku began to be appreciated as an autonomous seventeen-syllable verse form, his name still continued to be associated with it. Senryū himself seemed to prefer the retention of maeku, but even he could not stop the evolution of a new type of poem. Tsukeku in time became a completely independent genre, with his name firmly attached to it. Over two centuries after his death, the genre still lives on.

Verse Writing as a Game

Although maekuzuke as a poetry contest did not come into existence until the seventeenth century, Japanese poets from early times enjoyed themselves by exchanging or capping verses in a lighthearted mood. *Kojiki* (The Record of Ancient Matters, A.D. 712), Japan's oldest book, already contains an episode in which a prince asks a question in a verse of thirteen syllables and an old man responds in one of nineteen syllables. *Man'yōshū* (The Collection of Ten Thousand Leaves), a verse anthology compiled in the mid-eighth century, not only includes a number of dialogue poems but also records an instance in which two people join forces to compose a *waka* (also called tanka), a short verse with a 5–7–5–7–7 syllable pattern. Because waka flourished at the imperial court in the tenth and eleventh centuries, this kind of joint composition was frequently tried by noblemen and noblewomen in their relaxed moments, and in time examples of it found their way into the anthologies. To cite an example from *Shūishū* (The Collection of Gleanings, ca. 1000), a certain young woman who waited for her lover in vain one night expressed her disappointment in seventeen syllables:

at two in the morning

I finally learn what it means

to trust a man's heart

hitogokoro

ushimitsu ima wa

tanomaji yo

The lover, on reading the verse the following morning, apologized in fourteen syllables:

longing to see you in a dream

I slept—and slept too late

yume ni miyu ya to

ne zo suginikeru[3]

Other books of poems and tales that appeared in the tenth and eleventh centuries, such as *Ise monogatari* (Tales of Ise), *Yamato monogatari* (Tales of Yamato), and *Sanboku kikashū* (The Collection of Woodchips), also contain examples of collaborative composition. The fifth imperial verse anthology, *Kin'yōshū* (The Collection of Golden Leaves, 1127), even has a special section for poems written jointly by two poets.

The practice of composing poems in collaboration became so popular that in time it evolved into a new form of poetry called *renga* (linked verse). In renga, the first poet would write a hokku (opening verse) in a pattern of 5–7–5 syllables, which would be followed by a 7–7 syllable verse written by the second poet. The third participant would then contribute another seventeen-syllable verse, and the fourth another fourteen-syllable verse. In this way members of the group would take turns writing verses in seventeen and fourteen syllables alternately, usually until the sequence reached the one-hundredth verse. While the poets worked under a set of rules that ensured the artistic unity of the entire sequence, their greatest enjoyment lay in seeing the art of linkage manifesting itself one verse after another. Watching how the designated poet linked his verse to the previous one, other poets sighed in admiration or burst out laughing or vented their

[3] Shūishū, *poem no. 1184.*

unhappiness. Thus the standard renga anthologies, such as *Tsukubashū* (The Tsukuba Collection, 1356), do not present linked poems in their entirety but give selected sequences of two verses that show the art of linkage at its best. More than anything else, the compilers were interested in the ways two adjacent verses could be integrated with each other.

Renga had its heyday during the fourteenth and fifteenth centuries. Because most renga poets adored the aristocratic culture that had thrived at the imperial court in earlier centuries, their poetic ideals centered around an elegant, courtly type of beauty tinged with nostalgia. However, as time passed and the literacy rate rose among people outside the capital, an increasing number of those who had tastes of a different kind began to write poetry, and they wanted the realm of renga to be more inclusive in both theme and style. They were especially eager to see renga draw on more mundane subjects and use more colloquial expressions. Finally in the sixteenth century *haikai* (sportive verse) branched off from renga and established itself as a more plebeian form of group composition. It appealed to commoners, not only because it allowed down-to-earth topics and vernacular phrases, but also because it evinced earthy humor that was understood by everyone. Thus an early haikai anthology called *Inu Tsukubashū* (The Dog Tsukuba Collection, 1539?) contains the following two-verse sequence:

both the husband and the wife	*myōto nagara ya*
seem waiting for the nightfall	*yoru wo matsuran*
deep in their hearts	*makoto ni wa*
they feel that they haven't quite`	*mada uchitokenu*
patched up the quarrel	*nakanaori*[4]

---

[4] *Kanda Toyoho, ed.,* Teimon haikaishū *(Tokyo: Nihon Haisho Taikei Kankōkai, 1926), 44.*

The reader needs no knowledge of classical literature to appreciate this type of humor.

Haikai rapidly gained popularity among people of the plebeian class, especially after the society they lived in began to enjoy peace and prosperity in the early seventeenth century. It was in the last several decades of that century, however, that the world of haikai came to be polarized. That was because a poet of extraordinary talent, Matsuo Bashō (1644–1694), transformed haikai into serious poetry by refining its sportive elements, making it deeply reflective of man's relationship to nature. While a number of serious-minded poets became his followers, many others continued to prefer the earthier, more easily understood humor of earlier haikai. Those who taught haikai for a living especially had a need to attract students, and they wanted to keep haikai as an entertaining game that appealed to the average person. Various types of verse-writing games collectively known as *zappai* (miscellaneous haikai) were the result. Maekuzuke was none other than a variety of zappai.

In its origin, maekuzuke was an instructional method used by masters of renga and haikai. The teacher would compose a maeku consisting of fourteen or seventeen syllables and ask the student to write an appropriate tsukeku. He would then give a critique of the student's verse and suggest how it could be improved. When the teacher had more than one student, this teaching method would easily turn into a verse-writing contest. In the late seventeenth century it was made into a poetry contest open to the public and soon gained a number of enthusiastic fans, especially after prizes began to be given to the winners. According to a surviving record, a certain maekuzuke contest held in December 1693 received more than 10,600 entries sent by residents of fifteen different provinces. The compiler of a book published three years later observed: "The whole world is having fun by playing what is known as maekuzuke. There is no one, not even an aged woodcutter or a young reaper, who does not amuse himself with it."[5] To quote an example of early maekuzuke from a book published in 1702:

| it goes on forever | tsuzuki koso sure |
| it goes on forever | tsuzuki koso sure |

because of the blossoms	hana yue ni
another visitor today	kyō mo kyaku aru
at this grassy hut	kusa no io[6]

This example reveals that already at this early time the maeku was being made simple and repetitive so as to give maximum freedom to each prospective entrant's imagination. On the other hand, the tsukeku elicits no earthy humor; indeed, it echoes the Bashō school of haikai in its image of a poet-recluse.

Unfortunately, with the increased popularity of maekuzuke contests, many people with meager poetic talent declared themselves tenja. Anyone who knew a little about verse writing could become a master, since all he needed to do was come up with some maeku and distribute them to various poets' groups he knew. When the entries arrived, he would choose as many winning verses as he liked—or as many verses as there were prizes for—and announce the results. Such masters were interested more in gathering many verses (and the many entry fees that came with them) than in developing the poetic talents of the contestants; people with a real talent for poetry would write the more serious haikai anyway. Thus, in spite of the popularity of zappai in general and of maekuzuke in particular, few outstanding verses of this genre emerged be-

---

[5] *Kakujuken Yoshihiro, ed.*, Haikai takama no uguisu. *In* Tokugawa bungei ruijū *(Tokyo: Kokusho Kankōkai, 1914)*, 11:271.

[6] Momijigasa. *Quoted in Adachi Yoshio*, Edo senryū no shiteki kenkyū, *26*.

fore the mid-eighteenth century. There was a need for strong leadership that would change the situation. Fortunately, Karai Senryū made a timely appearance on the Japanese poetic scene to fill that need.

Karai Senryū and His Contributions

There are many possible reasons for the remarkable success of Karai Senryū as a maekuzuke master. First of all, Senryū was a perceptive reader of poetry with an excellent critical sense. He was also a conscientious referee who made the utmost effort to understand each entry and select the very best. It is reported that he dwelled long on a verse that puzzled him. His superior work as a contest judge was soon noticed by the more gifted regular entrants, and when they began to contribute their verses to his contests, others followed suit. His social position as the chief official of his ward also commanded a degree of public respect. He must have had good business sense, too, for his poetry contests had a slightly higher proportion of winners than those of other masters, while his entry fee was slightly lower.

More importantly, Senryū was better than other tenja at composing the kind of maeku that attracted entrants. Many of his maeku were so enticingly open-ended that they could not fail to stimulate the contestant's imagination. Furthermore, they were so simple that the tsukeku could be appreciated almost by themselves. In other words, even though his maeku contained fourteen syllables each (the seventeen-syllable maeku had fallen out of public favor by this time), they functioned as titles under which contestants were free to write whatever kind of poem they liked. And those "titles" were redolent of everyday life, on which everyone had some comment to make.

Lastly, the popularity of Senryū's poetry contests had to do with his predilection for Edo life and culture. Whereas many other masters accepted verses from the provinces, Senryū limited his clientele to his native city. During this period, the people of Edo were beginning to establish their cultural identity, an identity distinctly different from that of the Kyoto-Osaka area, admired for centuries by the rest of the nation. In contrast with the traditional sensibility that cherished an elegant, refined, opaque ideal of beauty, artists and men of letters in the newly rising city of Edo preferred a more vigorous, straightforward, down-to-earth style. They were also less ashamed of pursuing pleasure, especially carnal pleasure, and of giving it the kind of artistic expression that could be easily appreciated by the ordinary person. Senryū, born and reared in downtown Edo, was well aware of this new aesthetic trend. As a referee he aggressively selected verses expressing the tastes of a typical Edoite—an attitude that appealed to the civic pride of those who wrote verses for his contests.

It took some time, however, for Senryū to gain his reputation. His first maekuzuke contest, announced on September 27, 1757, received only 207 verses by the deadline date. The winning verses he chose totaled just 13. Undaunted, he held the second contest ten days later, and this time the submissions more than doubled, numbering 598. The third contest attracted 898 entries; the fourth, 1,261; the fifth, 1,614; and the sixth, 1,835. The increase was slow but steady. In a contest held in November 1762, the number of verses submitted finally exceeded ten thousand. Five years later, it went over twenty thousand. The record number of entries, reached at a contest held in November 1779 was 25,024. We wonder how Senryū was able to read all those verses. And he usually had only a short time to do so, since his regular contests were held at ten-day intervals during the autumn and winter of each year.

Senryū's rise to prominence as a maekuzuke master was helped by the publication of a verse anthology entitled *Yanagidaru* (The Willow Barrel) in 1765. The book was a collection of 756 verses selected from nearly ten thousand

winning entries in Senryū's contests, beginning with the
first contest in 1757 and covering the next seven years. The
finest ones selected by Senryū now became easily accessible to the general public. And in presenting them, the editor, Goryōken Arubeshi (?–1788), had adopted a refresh-
ing new policy to make reading easier: the book contained
tsukeku only, without maeku. Commenting on the policy,
Goryōken wrote in his preface: "In compiling this collection I have selected verses that could easily be understood
by themselves."[7] Tsukeku herewith took its first step toward becoming an independent poetic form, a form later
to be called "senryu." Goryōken himself, however, was interested less in its independence than in its relation to
contemporary haikai, for in his preface he also said he
wanted to tie a knot between them. In fact, he wanted to
elevate maekuzuke from the level of zappai, which was a
game, to the level of haikai, which was poetry. The title of
his anthology was apparently intended to signify such a
marriage between maekuzuke and haikai, for in those days
one of the standard gifts given to an engaged couple was a
barrel made of willow and filled with sake. The image of
a willow also hints at Senryū's name.

   Goryōken probably had many misgivings about the
public's reception of *Yanagidaru*, because dropping maeku was a daring experiment. But the reception turned out
to be extremely favorable, and the book became a best-
seller. The first edition had the word "complete" after the
title, indicating it was a one-time publication. Yet, as Goryōken was to recollect five years later, the publisher of the
book became so busy producing reprints that he had no
time to do anything else. Encouraged, Goryōken compiled *Yanagidaru 2* in 1767. Again it enjoyed a good sale.
From then on he brought out one volume each year, se-
lecting verses from contests held by Senryū during the preceding months. The success made Goryōken more con-

---

[7] *Okada Hajime, ed.,* Haifū yanagidaru zenshū, 1:3.

fident about his policy of omitting maeku. In his preface
to *Yanagidaru 5*, he proudly wrote: "The verses people
enjoy nowadays are the ones that are interesting in themselves, regardless of the way in which they are linked to
their maeku. This trend was started by me."[8]

It is not known to what extent Senryū, a close friend of
Goryōken's, participated in the compilation of *Yanagidaru*
or how much he liked the omission of maeku. The chang-
ing taste of the time, however, had to affect him and the
standards by which he screened entries. From the early
1770s, the verses he chose became more distinctly self-contained in meaning, even though he still retained the maeku
in his printed announcements of winning verses. For example, in one of his contests held in 1770, the maeku

a watchman has come   *aratamenikeri*
a watchman has come   *aratamenikeri*

inspired a contestant to think up the tsukeku

caught in the act   *shikarareta*
he flees, throwing away   *toko e utcharu*
a spray of blossoms   *hana no eda* (Y 7)

The two verses combined describe a little incident at a temple yard or some such place where many cherry trees are in
bloom. A visitor has just plucked some blossoms, when a
watchman suddenly appears on the scene. As the visitor
flees, he instinctively—or from a guilty conscience—tosses
away the stolen property, even though it is obvious that the
blossoms cannot be reattached to the tree. The two-verse
sequence skillfully captures a moment full of psychologi-
cal interest.

On the other hand, it might be observed that the maeku
is superfluous here, that the reader can derive the same
meaning from the tsukeku alone. As a matter of fact, the

[8] *Ibid.*, 1:99.

tsukeku without the maeku would give the reader's imagination more scope. The reader could, for instance, imagine a cherry tree blooming by a house and a passerby plucking a spray from it; the master of the house catches sight of the blossom-thief and shouts at him. The image of a guard in the maeku seems to fetter the reader's imagination.

Such examples abound in the contests of Senryū's later years. In some instances, the maeku appears to be not only unnecessary but almost irrelevant. The following example is from a contest held in 1771:

a thought crosses the mind   *omoi koso sure*
a thought crosses the mind   *omoi koso sure*

NO TRESPASSING—   *tōrinuke*
thanks to the sign, you find   *muyō de tōri-*
a shortcut   *nuke ga shire (Y 8)*

Definitely the second verse can stand by itself. Indeed, it has since become one of the better-known senryu, and today's readers have usually never heard of the maeku.

Senryū continued to hold contests regularly every autumn and winter (in later years he had special contests in other seasons as well), until he took to bed with a fatal illness in 1789. It is estimated that the number of winning verses he selected was well over seventy-five thousand. Goryōken also kept publishing *Yanagidaru* every year, until he fell ill in 1787. He died the following year, having compiled twenty-two volumes. After both Senryū and Goryōken were gone, their activities were taken over by others, but clearly the glory years had passed. Senryū's eldest son succeeded to his professional name at his death in 1790, yet Senryū II was a man of no special talent either as poet or as referee. He held no public contests; he merely attended the verse-writing parties of various poets' groups and made his selections, which were then published in subsequent volumes of *Yanagidaru*.

Goryōken's policy of having verses screened twice—first by the contest judge and then by the editor—was thereby broken. Also broken was the long-held practice of publishing one volume of *Yanagidaru* each year; now several volumes were brought out annually. The result was a marked increase in the proportion of mediocre verses. The reading public gradually lost interest in *Yanagidaru*, and its sales decreased. Senryū II was succeeded by Senryū III in 1818, and then by Senryū IV six years later, but these changes of leadership did not improve the situation. Finally, in 1838, *Yanagidaru* ceased publication. One hundred and sixty-seven volumes had appeared by then, but it has to be said that many of the verses worth reading are contained in the first twenty-four volumes, the ones that comprise the verses chosen by the original Senryū.

It would be wrong, however, to attribute the decline of senryu exclusively to lack of talent or effort on the part of those who succeeded Senryū. The decline had already started during his lifetime. The main reason lay in the brief verse form itself. With just seventeen syllables to work with, poets of later years found little room for creativity. And all the subjects they could find had already been treated by their predecessors in every conceivable way. Consequently they tried to compete with each other in either bookish allusion or technical finesse. The result was an increase in verses that were overintellectualized, pedantic, or enigmatic, with little or no emotional appeal. The following example, taken from *Yanagidaru* 22 (1788), will illustrate the point:

of the Three	*sannin de*
only one is eating a fish	*hitori uo kū*
this autumn nightfall	*aki no kure*

Few Japanese readers today, except scholars in classical poetry, would be able to understand the poem without a footnote. "The Three" refers to three medieval poets, the

priest Saigyō (1118–1190), the priest Jakuren (?–1202), and
Fujiwara Teika (1161–1241), known as the authors of the
three finest waka on the subject of autumn nightfall. Because those who had entered the priesthood were forbidden to eat fish, only Teika was able to have it for dinner.
The author's point is novel, and there is humorous incongruity in the image of an elegant court poet eating a fish
dinner. But the verse reeks of pedantry.

Still other factors contributed to the decline of senryu.
A type of popular fiction known as *kibyōshi* (yellowback),
featuring the same type of humor as senryu, began to attract the general reader in 1775, with the publication of
Kinkin-sensei eiga no yume (Master Kinkin Has a Dream
of Glory). *Kyōka* (mad waka), a parodic and satirical verse
form containing thirty-one syllables, suddenly exploded
on the Edo poetic scene in the 1880s, as Ōta Shokusanjin
(1749–1823) made his appearance. Alarmed by the popularity of satirical literature, the shogunate issued a series of
ordinances restricting freedom of publication, beginning
in 1790. The censorship was such that when the publishers of *Yanagidaru* brought out a new edition around 1800,
they had to go over the first twenty-nine volumes and cut
out some satirical verses. With all these factors combined,
there was no way in which senryu could have regained the
vitality of the former years. And it did not, at least for the
rest of the premodern period.

Authors of Premodern Senryu

Little is known about the identities of those who wrote senryu in premodern Japan. That is because of the way
maekuzuke contests were conducted. When someone submitted a verse to a contest, he did not send it directly to the
referee. Instead, he handed it over to the secretary of the
poets' group that he belonged to, or that was located in his
neighborhood. At the contest deadline, the secretary gath-

ered all the verses, crossed out the authors' names (or, more likely, copied out the verses without the names), and then forwarded them to the tenja. This procedure was to ensure the fairness of the contest. Therefore, when the referee posted printed sheets announcing the winners, the verses were accompanied only by the names of the poets' groups. Presumably the prizes were sent to the groups' secretaries, who then delivered them to the individual authors.

Karai Senryū stuck strictly to this procedure throughout his life as he conducted his regular contests in autumn and winter. In later years, however, he seems to have been less strict when he refereed off-season contests. *Yanagidaru* includes some of the authors' names from its ninth volume onward. However, because those names are pseudonyms, their identities are unknown in most instances. Senryū himself may have written some senryu, but none is known today.

There do remain some documents suggesting what kind of people the authors were. One is an essay entitled *Nemonogatari* (Mutterings in Bed), in which a number of those who wrote senryu in the 1830s are talked about. One such person, who wrote verses under the pseudonym Sanshō, is described as follows:

> He makes his living as a day laborer. Although he is neither a drinker nor a smoker, he is so devoted to verse writing all the year round that he cannot afford to buy new clothes. His interests include not only senryu but also hokku, haikai, and kyōka. He participates in all kinds of verse-writing contests, always ending up as a loser.[9]

Other senryu writers mentioned in the essay include three firemen, two professional storytellers, a landlord, a stew-

---

[9] *Quoted in Mayama Seika, "Tenpō-goro no senryū sakusha." In* Mayama Seika zuihitsu senshū *(Tokyo: Dainihon Yūbenkai Kōdansha, 1952), 3:181.*

ard, an ivory sculptor, an embroiderer, a tavern owner, a noodle shop operator, a lantern seller, a cook, a plasterer, a Zen monk, and a friar. Another essay, *Ensai Kanō no shuki* (Ensai Kanō's Notes, 1855), also refers to contemporary senryu writers; they include two physicians, two publishers, two fish vendors, and a clerk for the municipal government. From other documents it is also known that the kabuki actor Ichikawa Danjūrō VII (1741–1806), the ukiyo-e artist Katsushika Hokusai (1760–1849), and the fiction writer Ryūtei Tanehiko (1783–1842) wrote senryu. From all this evidence it can be deduced that many of those who wrote senryu were people of the plebeian class, a conclusion entirely consistent with the thoughts and feelings expressed in a great many premodern senryu surviving today.

On the other hand, there is evidence indicating that a number of samurai participated in senryu contests, too. Many poets' groups that sent verses to maekuzuke contests were located in districts of Edo where the majority of residents belonged to the warrior class. Roughly one half of Edo's population consisted of samurai anyway, and the literacy rate was highest in their class. Although it is true that most senryu take a townsman's point of view, it has to be remembered that a low-ranking samurai led a life not too different from a commoner's. In fact, some samurai were that in name only, as they earned their living by doing the kinds of work commoners did. Unemployed samurai, known as *rōnin*, led a life even harder than an ordinary townsman's.

It seems that even high-ranking samurai read and wrote senryu, though they were usually reluctant to admit it. For instance Matsuura Seizan (1760–1841), a feudal lord who had a fief in Kyushu, made frequent reference to senryu in his essays collectively called *Kasshi yawa* (Night Chattings Beginning on Kasshi Day, 1821–1841). He was a man well educated in the more serious branches of learning such as Confucianism and classical literature, yet he had to concede: "Although verses of Senryū's school are crude, I ad-

mire the penetrating observations they make on the nature
of man and the world."[10] While he says nothing about trying his hand in writing senryu, it is surmised, at least by
one modern scholar, that he wrote more than two hundred verses in that form.[11] Another man of the ruling warrior class who is thought to have written senryu outranks
even Seizan. He is Tayasu Munetake (1715–1771), a shogun's son and one of the major waka poets of the eighteenth century. Apparently he entered a verse in one of
Senryū's contests in 1764. To the maeku

| what happy timing! | *yoi kagen nari* |
| what happy timing! | *yoi kagen nari* |

Munetake came up with the tsukeku

the paper weight—	*keisan ga*
just when it returns to its sheath	*fukuro ni iru to*
warm sake is ready	*kan ga deki*[12]

A paper weight is needed when one writes a letter with a
brush. This tsukeku, combined with the maeku, skillfully
suggests the author's relief on having completed a long
letter that had been difficult to write. The verse, however, is not included in *Yanagidaru*, probably because its
meaning is not sufficiently self-contained.

It appears that few women wrote senryu. That is no
wonder, since in those days it was considered a little unla-
dylike for a woman even to write haikai. Ladies were expected to learn waka, a verse form traditionally thought to
be more elegant and feminine. Senryu is less elegant than

[10] *Matsuura Seizan,* Kasshi yawa *(Tokyo: Kokusho Kankōkai, 1910),*
2:414.
[11] *Nakamura Yukihiko, "Kaisetsu." In Nakamura Yukihiko and Na-*
kano Mitsutoshi, eds., Kasshi yawa *(Tokyo: Heibonsha, 1977–*
78), 6: 433.
[12] *Quoted in Kanda Bōjin,* Edo senryū wo tanoshimu, *124.*

haikai, far less so than waka. Still, later volumes of *Yanagi-daru* do include verses by several women poets, who had such strange pseudonyms as Uyū (Crow's Friend), Tessen (Steel Fan), and Bungyo (Literate Fish). Although their identities are unknown, the fact that the editors specifically noted their gender in the book is itself proof of how rare it was for a woman to write senryu.

The Nature and Value of Premodern Senryu

It would be difficult to claim that senryu written in premodern Japan is great poetry, no matter how we may propose to measure the greatness of a poem. For Edo townsmen of the eighteenth century, senryu was more entertainment than poetry. *Yanagidaru* had a good sale each year because the verses it contained amused a vast number of people, including those who had no special interest in literature. Those who wished to write more serious poetry could—and did—utilize other types of verse, such as haikai and waka. Yosa Buson (1716–1784), the greatest haikai poet of the eighteenth century, proclaimed a poetic principle known as *rizoku* or "detachment from the mundane," precisely because senryu and much of haikai in his time seemed too mundane for his poetic taste. Kobayashi Issa (1763–1827), who had a more worldly mind than Buson and who may have written some senryu in his youth, went on to focus his creative energy on haikai and ended up becoming a major poet in that genre. As mentioned before, the waka poet Tayasu Munetake wrote senryu, yet he did so merely to amuse himself.

At least three reasons can be thought of to explain why senryu was less appealing than other verse forms to the most gifted poets of the time. First, whereas hokku, which had the same 5–7–5 syllable pattern as senryu, could create poetic tension by the technique of internal comparison, senryu, lacking such an established device, could not easily do so and too often allowed itself to be flat and prosaic. Also, it was too short to make itself as lyrically moving as waka or as tonally multifarious as linked verse. Second, while a haikai poet could create semantic complexity through the use of *kigo* (season word), a senryu writer had no such culturally loaded vocabulary at his disposal and had to devise his own method if he wanted to write a verse that would expand in meaning. He could use a word referring to the season (and there are many instances of such use, as seen in the eighth section of this anthology), but because senryu had no tradition of seasonal poetry to feed on, the word would not carry the kind of rich cultural connotations that a kigo would. Third, senryu's thematic focus on social life led its writers to observe people primarily in the context of the contemporary society, not in terms of a more transcendental principle. It did treat foibles of human nature, but only when those foibles manifested themselves in everyday social behavior. To overgeneralize a little, very likely a poet moved by the beauty of nature would write a hokku. A poet wishing to vent out a personal emotion like love or grief would compose a waka. Someone with a novelist's eye but without his ability (or patience) to construct a lengthy plot jotted down senryu.

The raison d'étre of senryu, then, lies in its value as popular literature, literature for mass production and consumption. If it is poetry, it is the kind of poetry specifically intended to entertain the millions. It belongs to the type of "light verse" as defined by W. H. Auden: poetry that has "for its subject matter the everyday social life of its period or the experiences of the poet as an ordinary human being."[13] Such poetry has to be "light" or humorous; otherwise the general public would show no interest in it. No one in premodern Japan tried to give a scholarly definition of senryu,

---

[13] W. H. Auden, "Introduction." In The Oxford Book of Light Verse (Oxford: Clarendon Press, 1938), ix.

but an essayist named Ogawa Akimichi (1737–1815) once made a comment touching on its basic nature. In his opinion, senryu is "playful verse that comments on human behaviors, virtues and vices, noble and base emotions, thoughts of upper- and lower-class people, and all the other matters that make up this life on earth."[14] The key word here is "playful verse" (*zareku*). Senryu was comic verse, a type of verse that gained enormous popularity through its humorous quality, through its ability to make the reader laugh. Edo townsmen amused themselves by reading and writing senryu, not caring whether it qualified as poetry.

In making their verse humorous and entertaining, senryu writers in premodern Japan often depended on the mechanisms of laughter widely observable in Western culture and variously theorized by Western philosophers. Indeed, if the humor of senryu somehow comes through in English translation, it is because senryu writers frequently used the instruments of laughter commonly employed in the Western world. Unfortunately, the subject matter to which those instruments were applied is closely related to the mores of the contemporary society, making the humor of senryu difficult to understand for those who know little about social customs in premodern Japan.

The oldest known mechanism of laughter in the West is built around a feeling of superiority. Briefly stated, philosophers like Plato, Aristotle, and Hobbes thought that we laugh from our feeling of mingled superiority and triumph, the kind of feeling that comes to us when we discover incompetence, clumsiness, misfortune, or misjudgment in others. As is well known, Aristotle defined comic heroes as the "persons worse than the average" because they make us feel superior by comparison. Knowing nothing about Aristotle's theory, Karai Senryū seemed to think along the same line when he specified the kind of people he thought were

---

[14] *Ogawa Akimichi*, Chirizukabanashi. *In Iwamoto Sashichi, ed.,* Enseki jisshu *(Tokyo: Kokusho Kankōkai, 1907–1908), 1:274.*

most suitable for subjects of senryu. Appearing in the sequence of verses published at the end of *Yanagidaru 2*, these
subjects include illiterates, loafers, parasites, fanatics, in-
valids, blind men, low-ranking samurai, destitute samurai,
concubines, men with idiosyncrasies, and so forth.

Of the people listed above, senryu writers seem to have
been especially fond of ridiculing people of the ruling warrior class. Perhaps because townsmen were always looked
down upon by samurai in their daily life, they made extra
efforts to find weaknesses in the latter and made them a
source of their laughter. Financially better off, they would
jeer at the low-ranking samurai's poverty:

a last resort:	*tamashii wo*
the samurai puts his soul	*seppa zumatte*
in pawn	*shichi ni oki (Y 39)*

Bushidō, the Way of the Warrior by which a samurai was
to conduct his life, taught that his sword should be treasured as if it were his very soul. The samurai's high ethical
standards, however, had to yield to material need when he
and his family were starving. The senryu implies the triumph of the Way of the Townsman over Bushidō.

If the senryu cited above is read as satire, its humor
could also be analyzed in terms of Bergson's idea of "mechanical inelasticity." According to Bergson, the ridicu-
lous is something mechanical and inflexible that has become encrusted, as it were, upon the living, which seeks
to be pliant and free. The Way of the Warrior, which was
meaningful in a war-torn society, has become a kind of en-
crustation on samurai life in peacetime, but the shogun's
government does not grasp that fact and keeps on promoting it. Another senryu

samurai's quarrel	*mononofu no*
doesn't end, until it produces	*kenka ni goke ga*
two widows	*futari deki (Y 4)*

also mocks at the samurai's inelastic mindset that would not allow him to swallow his pride and arrive at a compromise without bloodshed. Of course, this kind of mental rigidity was not confined to samurai; it pervaded people of all classes and occupations, providing fitting material for senryu writers.

Bergson's influential theory of laughter led later thinkers to develop some interesting variations of it, each of which sees laughter as man's attempt to assert his vitality and animal drives in the face of social prohibitions and constraints. Mikhail Bakhtin, for instance, traced the origin of comic and parodic literature to the festivities associated with the carnival, where temporarily liberated people laughed away the authorities of church and state. Susanne K. Langer also believed that laughter arose from a surge of vital feeling, a flash of victorious self-assertion amid the alien and impartial chances of the world. Although Bakhtin's theory was mainly concerned with the novel, and Langer's with drama, their underlying ideas that emphasize man's vitality help us to understand the nature of laughter evoked by some senryu, such as:

"All is void," he says	*shikisokuze-*
and sets out on a side trip	*kū toburai*
from the funeral site	*kara soreru* (Y 77)

"All is void" is a well-known Buddhist dictum teaching the illusory nature of all things on earth, including human life. The man in this senryu is reminded of the dictum because he has just attended the funeral of someone he knew. He reacts to the dictum immediately after the funeral: instead of going straight home, he takes a "side trip," which, as the contemporary reader knew, means a trip to the pleasure quarters. Such a trip, jokingly called *shōjin otoshi* (the end-of-abstinence rite), was a common practice among the young men of the time. If a comedy is structured around the upset and recovery of the protagonist's rhythm of life (as Langer says), the mourner in this senryu must be said to be a comic hero because by performing the "rite" he is re-asserting his vitality that has been suppressed during the days leading up to the funeral.

The mechanism of laughter in the senryu cited above may also be explained by another influential theory of humor known as the incongruity theory. Proposed by such philosophers as Kant, Schopenhauer, and Kierkegaard, the theory argues that what amuses us is some object of perception that contradicts what we normally expect of it. In the example above, the religious maxim "All is void" is unexpectedly followed by a description of an action that is anything but religious. Similar examples abound in pre-modern senryu. The following verse describes a young woman who was recently married:

not a word   *ichigon mo*
she spoke, yet the house   *iwazu nyōbo no*
has become the wife's   *uchi ni nari (YS 18)*

When she first came to his house, she was a shy, blushing bride who could hardly speak a word to him. In a matter of weeks, however, she has somehow taken complete control of his household, though she still does not say much.

The incongruity theory also has produced a number of variations. Kant, for example, found the cause of laughter in sudden dissipation of a strained expectation and cited a humorous episode about a certain heir preparing a funeral for his rich relative. As Kant tells us, the heir had diffi-culty arranging a solemn ceremony because "the more money I give my mourners to look grieved, the more cheerful they look."[15] This type of comic incongruity is found in senryu also. The following verse comes especial-ly close to Kant's example:

[15] *Immanuel Kant,* The Critique of Judgment, *trans. Werner S. Pluhar (Indianapolis: Hackett, 1987), 204.*

professional smile   *aisō ni*
of the mortician's wife: *koshiya no naigi*
a look of grief   *beso wo kaki (YS 3)*

Even more common in senryu is incongruity as conceived
by Schopenhauer, who saw the essence of humor in the
disharmony between what we know in theory and what we
see in actuality. A mismatch of ideal and reality is pre-
sented in a senryu like:

shares in a teahouse   *chayakabu ga*
among the legacies   *sen sōjō no*
of the late bishop   *katami nari (Y 7)*

Senryu writers frequently induced satirical laughter by
sketching amorous priests, mercenary physicians, and corrupt officials, because they saw a wide gap between the
concept of such professions and their knowledge of those
professionals' actual behavior.

    The incongruity theory could usefully be applied to the
senryu collected in the ninth section of this anthology,
which portray famous heroes of the past caught in un-
heroic situations or observed from a realistic point of view.
The theory helps to explain the humor of parodic senryu,
too, for parody creates comic incongruity between the
original and the imitation. Pun, wit, irony, and double entendre often involve other kinds of laughable incongruity,
and all are utilized in senryu. To quote an example of double entendre:

how beautiful   *rippa naru*
she looks—a bride   *mono hanayome no*
with nothing on   *maruhadaka (Y 10)*

"A bride with nothing on" refers to *hadakayome*, meaning
a bride who brings no dowry with her. The underlying
idea is that a beautiful woman can get married without a

dowry, whereas a homely one has difficulty finding a husband even when her parents are rich. But, of course, readers are likely to interpret the verse at another, more literal
level on first reading; that is just the point.

Although many philosophers today seem to favor the
incongruity theory in analyzing humor, some who are
more psychologically oriented want to see laughter as a result of relieved tension. According to Spencer, Freud and,
as we saw, Bakhtin, laughter occurs when a forbidden
thought or feeling is freed from its repressed state. The
theory can be applied to explain the humor inherent in a
number of premodern senryu, for Edo townsmen who
wrote those verses lived in a feudal, regimented society
and had to supress a great deal of what they thought and
felt in their daily life. Reading or writing senryu provided
an outlet—a safety valve, as Freud might have said—for
those suppressed thoughts and feelings. Many senryu satirizing samurai, priests, doctors, and government officials
can be considered substitute for physical aggression. One
of the best-known premodern senryu falls in this category:

the official's little son—	*yakunin no*
how fast he's learned to open	*ko wa niginigi wo*
and close his fist!	*yoku oboe (Y 1)*

Babies mimic what their parents do. This little son has
learned to open and close his fist at a very early age because
he watches his father receiving bribes day in and day out.
The verse, first published in *Yanagidaru* 1, was dropped
from later editions for fear of government censure.

The relief theory also helps to account for the abundance of erotic senryu. Carnal desire is a most deeply root-
ed feeling, yet its expression is inhibited to varying degrees
in all cultures. Although Japanese society in the eighteenth century was in many ways more tolerant in sexual
matters than our society is today, people still had to be reserved in talking about sex. Senryu provided one of the

means for Edo townsmen to let such feelings out. Thus there is a multitude of senryu peppered with slang words for male and female genitals as well as for various bedroom practices used by courtesans. There were so many such senryu that someone collected them in an anthology; entitled *Suetsumuhana* (The Saffron Flower), it appeared in four volumes between 1776 and 1801. Many of these senryu violate our sense of decency—or, at least, I lack the skill to translate them without perhaps offending some readers. I submit the following example only because it uses a euphemism for a word that is normally shunned in respectable poetic language:

the moon makes her grieve	*tsuki mireba*
over thousands of things—	*chiji ni kanashiki*
His Lordship's widow	*gokōshitsu (K 3)*

The poem humorously alludes to a waka by Ōe Chisato (fl. 897–903) that is renowned for its expression of the vague melancholy felt by a sensitive person looking at the autumn moon:

the moon makes me muse	*tsuki mireba*
over thousands of things	*chiji ni mono koso*
that sadden my heart	*kanashikere*
even though I know autumn	*waga mi hitotsu no*
does not come to my life alone	*aki ni wa aranedo*[16]

The first two lines of the senryu present a sensitive person gazing upon the autumn moon and pondering over many sad things, just like the speaker in Chisato's waka. Yet the last line indicates that the person is a widow, and that fact would have reminded the contemporary reader that the word "moon" (*tsuki*) is also a euphemism for a woman's menstrual period. The widow is still young, and promi-

---

[16] Kokin waka shū, *poem no. 193.*

nent among "thousands of things" she remembers is the time she spent with her husband in the bedroom.

It can be said, then, that Western theories of laughter help to uncover the mechanism of humor at work in a large majority of senryu. Yet, as with any theories, they leave out exceptions. Predictably, the exceptions seem to have something to do with the peculiarities of Japanese culture in general or of the senryu form in particular.

There are, for instance, a sizable number of senryu that provoke nonaggressive kinds of laughter. Laughter in Western theories usually includes an element of aggression. "Laughter, by withholding pity, can serve as a weapon," says Norman N. Holland. "We use it as a social corrective. We attack individuals, types, institutions, even deities by laughing at them."[17] Yet many senryu on children do not laugh at them; they laugh with them. For example, the humor in the senryu

the toddler	*hainarau*
struggling to get a handle	*ko no hone wo oru*
on a melon	*uri hitotsu (K 1)*

does not seem to accommodate any of the Western theories referred to above. The superiority theory will not do, since what we feel toward the little child is not scorn but affection. Asō Isoji, one of the few Japanese scholars who have tried to analyze the humor of senryu, called this *junshin na warai* (innocent laughter) or *jaki no nai warai* (laughter without malice) and considered it characteristic of senryu.[18] For examples of poets who evoked a similar type of laughter, he cited the Zen monk Ikkyū (1394–1481) and the haikai poet Bashō, who also had an interest in Zen. R. H. Blyth, who has translated more senryu into

---

[17] *Norman N. Holland,* Laughing: A Psychology of Humor *(Ithaca: Cornell University Press, 1982), 17.*

[18] *Asō Isoji,* Warai no kenkyū, *472–73.*

English than anyone else, also thought that the verses selected by Karai Senryū have "the taste of Zen" to a certain degree.[19] We have to be cautious in seeking a connection between senryu and Zen, however, since the all-pervasive nature of Zen Buddhism enables us to find a manifestation of its spirit in almost anything we want. On the other hand, we cannot completely ignore the fact that senryu is a product of Japanese culture, which was under the influence of Zen in medieval times.

Then there are some senryu on children that contain so much affection or sympathy that they elicit little or no laughter. Instead of withholding pity, they express it without reserve. The result is senryu without humor. For instance, here is an observation about a young girl who is entering adolescence:

when she starts to feel	*hazukashisa*
coy, she enters a woman's life	*shitte onna no*
so full of pain	*ku no hajime (Y 1)*

In all likelihood the writer of this verse was male, but he fully understood the hard life women in feudal times were forced to endure after coming of age. The verse does contain an unexpected juxtaposition between feeling bashful and women's life in general, an incongruity that might have led to humor in other contexts. In this instance, however, the weight of the general statement on women's lives is so heavy, and the speaker's sympathy for the young girl is so deep, that the seed of humor does not germinate. This senryu is more an epigram than a comic verse.

At a polar opposite from those verses brimming with affection and sympathy, there are some senryu that seem to contain a good deal of malice. Naturally they provoke derisive, ill-natured laughter. Oftentimes, however, the malice implied in their laughter is directed toward the authors

[19] R. H. *Blyth*, Japanese Life and Character in Senryū, 9.

themselves as well as toward their targets. Our laughter fizzles out in midcourse, when the full impact of the verse hits home. Here is an example:

the chef	*ryōrinin*
while he sharpens his knife	*togu uchi koi wo*
leaves the carp swimming	*oyogaseru (Y 3)*

If we could laugh at the ignorance of the poor carp, we would be able to apply the superiority theory to this verse. But when we realize that we ourselves could be the carp, our sense of superiority vanishes. If there is humor in this senryu, it is black humor.

Another type of laughter that seems unique to senryu has to do with semantic ambiguity. Senryu is not as open-ended as hokku or haiku, which was originally the first stanza of a longer poem. Still, it consists of only seventeen syllables and has to leave a considerable amount of blank space in sketching the subject, consequently forcing readers to use their imagination to fill in the blank. In other words, senryu is a type of comic poetry in which the laughter it induces may change its character with individual readers. Of course, that is true of any laughable thing, as laughing is a subjective response to a certain kind of stimulus. But a brief verse form like senryu allows a greater degree of subjectivity on the respondent's part. A simple example would be the verse

"All women. . ."	*subete onna*
he begins, and then	*to iu mono to*
glances around	*sokora wo mi (Y 9)*

which asks the reader to supply the words that might come after "All women." What the speaker is about to tell the listener—obviously a male—is something that should not be heard by a woman, but what could that be? Each reader is invited to build a story around the senryu by identifying

the speaker and the listener, locating them in a specific situation, and completing the speaker's sentence.

Another ambiguous, but not so simple, senryu is:

the Zen monk	*Zenshū wa*
done with his meditation	*zazen ga sumu to*
looks for fleas	*nomi wo tori (Y 2)*

The humor of this verse seems analyzable through the
incongruity theory, for here is a somber, dignified Zen
monk engaged in a trivial act: catching fleas. Or we
might apply the superiority theory and laugh at the monk
who has tried to endure the itch all through his long
meditation. But, on the other hand, surely Zen Buddhism emphasizes the importance of the ordinary and
the trivial. Does it not erase the border between the spiritual and the physical? Why should the essence of Zen
not be found in a flea? Is there any real difference between meditating in a Zen posture and hunting for fleas?
Such are the questions that the verse's ambiguity acti-
vates in the reader's mind.

In the final analysis, it appears that the humorous effects of senryu are too varied for any broad generalizations.
Perhaps the word laughter itself is too limited in connota-
tion to define the effects, for there seem to be cases where
such terms as smile, grin, and sneer fit better. Some senryu do not induce any emotion approaching amusement,
especially for today's readers whose sensibilities differ considerably from Edo townsmen's. We have to study these
verses in the light of scholarly annotations before we understand what they mean or why they are funny.

For that very reason, however, premodern senryu gives
us a good deal of insight into the society and people that
produced it. By studying senryu, we come to know the
mores of the contemporary society to which its humor is
closely related. We learn how ordinary people of the time
thought and felt, their attitudes and values, the way they

looked at life. To be sure, that is the prime value of all popular literature, and eighteenth-century Japan had such
plebeian literary genres as haikai, kyōka, kabuki, and
kibyōshi in addition to senryu. Yet authors who worked in
those genres were the more-educated members of the society, even though they wrote for popular taste. Senryu
was written by the nonelite, including plasterers, fishmon-
gers, and day laborers. Unlike the other genres it did not
identify authorship, and that practice also helped its writers to be more honest with themselves when they expressed their thoughts and feelings. If popular literature
offers us "a window upon a world of ordinary men and women in the past," as Victor E. Neuburg says,[20] premodern
senryu as popular literature provides a very large window
indeed, for more than 200,000 such verses have been pre-
served for our reading and enjoyment.

Senryu in Modern Japan

With the Meiji Restoration of 1868, Western culture began
to flow freely into Japan. The poetry of Europe, with its
rich intellectual content and great freedom of form, so
dazzled the Japanese that they came to look down upon
their own poetic heritage. Even Western poetry apart, the
contemporary senryu seemed trite, stereotyped, and not
worth reading. The verse form had lost its vitality because
those who wrote it had to endure a stifling environment
created by the nationwide senryu hierarchy. They had to
work within many rigid rules imposed by the leaders of the
established system, who claimed to be heirs to Karai Senryū. No one could serve as a tenja unless he had official
permission from Senryū V, or VI, or VII, or whoever was
atop the system at the time. Under such circumstances,

---

[20] Victor E. Neuburg, Popular Literature: A History and Guide
(New York: Penguin Books, 1977), 12.

there was no way in which spirited verse satirizing the authorities could be written.

The first step toward the modernization of senryu was taken by writers completely outside the hierarchy. They were journalists who wanted to lampoon current political and social affairs through poetic satire, and they found the senryu form lying conveniently at hand. Just ten years after the Restoration, the weekly *Maru maru chinbun* (Cheerful Cheerful News Report) started a column to which anyone could contribute a seventeen-syllable poem that humorously commented on a hot topic of the day. The column received entries from a number of people who had previously had nothing to do with senryu and who, unrestricted by tradition, were not slow to satirize. The following is typical:

with earthworms for bait   *yōgakusha*
scholars in Western learning   *mimizu wo esa ni*
fish for an office   *kan wo tsuri*[21]

The earthworms are a metaphor for script written in Roman letters. The Japanese government at the time was in desperate need of people who had some proficiency in English, German, or French.

The more conscious effort to modernize senryu was started by two journalists, who initially worked for the daily newspaper *Nippon*. Sakai Kuraki (1869–1945), who studied poetry with Masaoka Shiki (1867–1902), launched a senryu reform movement under the influence of his teacher, who had helped to modernize haikai and waka. In 1903 he published *Senryū kōgai* (The Outline of Senryu), promoting restoration of the free spirit of senryu displayed in the early volumes of *Yanagidaru*. However, his greater interest in premodern Japanese culture than in current political affairs alienated the editors of *Nippon*, and he had to leave the newspaper. His successor, Inoue

---

[21] Maru maru chinbun 94 *(February 8, 1879).*

Kenkabō (1870–1934), was more attuned to political and
social trends. His new column, called "Shindai yanagidaru" (Yanagidaru on Modern Topics), encouraged senryu writers to take up topics characteristic of the emerging
new society. His policy was warmly welcomed by the readers of the newspaper: less than one year after the inaugu-
ration of the column, the number of contributors had increased to more than three hundred.

Heartened by this success, Kenkabō started a magazine called *Senryū* in 1904. His rival Kuraki, who had by
then become the editor of a senryu column in another
newspaper, founded the senryu journal *Satsukigoi* (May
Carp) the following year. That was only the beginning.
Those who tasted the pleasure of writing senryu for these
columns began organizing themselves into groups all
over Japan, many of them starting their own magazines.
By 1912, the number of such magazines published in
Japan had reached fifty. Many major newspapers, week-
lies, and monthlies also came to devote some space to
their readers' senryu. The trend accelerated with time so
that, in 1935, of more than two hundred national and
local newspapers the ones that did not have a senryu column totaled only twelve.

As the public interest in senryu increased, there appeared a number of new theories attempting to define its
essence. Varied as they were, those theories can be said to
have ranged between the two extreme poles of Marxism
and art for art's sake. The latter had its beginning in 1910,
when the senryu magazine *Shin senryū* (New Senryu)
started a column for free verse. The column's editors, led
by Anzai Ichian (1868–?) and Andō Genkaibō (1880–1928),
maintained that senryu should be poetry before it was senryu, and they saw no essential difference between haiku,
senryu, and short free verse. Their position was extended
in the direction of symbolism and surrealism by Tanaka
Gorohachi (1895–1937), who believed that the realm of
senryu "lies in the area of life that cannot be glimpsed

through prose composition."[22] However, most of his verses, like the example below, followed the conventional
5–7–5 syllable pattern:

holding	*tenjō no*
some heavenly secret	*himitsu wo daite*
a star leaps	*hoshi ga tobi*[23]

Kimura Hanmonsen (1889–1953) went farther than
Gorohachi and wrote free verse like the following, which
he called senryu:

in the sunset glow	*yūyake no naka no*
a slaughterhouse:	*togyūjō*
cow cow cow cow cow	*ushi ushi ushi ushi ushi*
cow cow cow cow cow	*ushi ushi ushi ushi ushi*[24]

It is not known how many followers this type of verse
gained at the time, but it appealed to poets who had been
tired of many contemporary senryu that merely poked fun
at trivial incidents.

At the other extreme, those with left-wing beliefs tried
to invigorate senryu by using it to promote socialism and
communism. Their activities were part of the general proletarian literary movement that swept Japan in the 1920s,
but the type of verse they wrote was bound to emerge
sooner or later as long as senryu writers were not blind to
the ills of a modern capitalist society. The social conse-
quences of the severe depression that hit Japan after World
War I were obvious to anyone. There were also signs indicating that modernized Japan, increasingly under the control of militarists, ultra-nationalists, and big business, was

[22] *Tanaka Gorohachi, "Shakaishugi geijutsu no hihan." Quoted in
Kusumoto Kenkichi and Yamamura Yū, Shin senryū e no shōtai,
118.*
[23] *Quoted in Saitō Daiyū, Gendai senryū nyūmon, 156.*
[24] *Quoted in Bitō Sanryū, Senryū nyūmon, 125.*

steadily moving toward an expansionist war. Thus some senryu writers joined other poets and novelists in attacking the establishment from a leftist point of view. Their leader was Morita Katsuji (1892–1979), an employee of the National Railways, who wrote a senryu like:

a labor strike—	*sutoraiki*
the chain is loosened	*isshaku kusari*
by a few inches	*nobasareru*[25]

The most fearless of the proletarian senryu writers was a young factory worker named Tsuru Akira (1909–1938), who wrote some daring antiwar verses at the time when Japan was engaged in a war with China. Below is one of the six sequential senryu he wrote in 1937:

no arms or legs—	*te to ashi wo*
they turned the man into a log	*moida maruta ni*
before sending him home	*shite kaeshi*[26]

In the government's eyes, this and other five senryu in the sequence had gone too far. He was arrested by the authorities; a few months later, he died in jail.

Censorship became even more severe after Japan entered World War II in 1941. No work of senryu, or of any genre of literature for that matter, could be published unless it explicitly promoted the government's wartime policies. The end of the war in August 1945, therefore, came as a relief for most senryu writers. Their reaction was immediate. Nearly twenty senryu groups were founded, or resumed activities, between August and December of that year. In 1946 some fifty more groups were formed, with headquarters located all over the country. Within the next few years, dozens of senryu magazines were in

---

[25] *Quoted in Kusumoto and Yamamura, 175.*
[26] *Quoted in Bitō, 100.*

circulation. Daily newspapers and weekly magazines continued to publish senryu, now with little fear of government intervention.

What characterized senryu after World War II was, above all, a thematic and stylistic diversity that reflected the chaos of postwar society. All the ideologies that had informed Japanese codes of conduct before and during the war were now considered outdated, reactionary, and evil, as the country lay devastated both physically and spiritually. Starting from scratch, leaders of senryu groups had to formulate new theories of poetic composition to fit a social reality that was going through unprecedented changes. Editors of the magazine *Senryū kenkyū* (Senryu Studies), for instance, chose to stress the importance of displaying the author's individuality. *Senba*, published in the Senba district of Osaka, advocated "romantic senryu" filled with youthful lyricism, while *Senryū*, a magazine based in Tokyo, promoted the spirit of haiku in senryu. *Jinmin senryū* (People's Senryu) revived the proletarian movement and encouraged contributors to write verses with left-wing implications. *Tōkyō senryū*, despite the fact that it was edited by Senryū XVI (1888–1977), took a radical stand and promoted free-style senryu. Many other magazines with many other editorial policies came out one after another, giving senryu writers a wide range of choice in theme and style.

It must be said, however, that with all that diversity senryu in the postwar period did not go to the farthest extremes as it had before the war. Few senryu were as radically imagistic as Hanmonsen's or as militantly leftist as Tsuru Akira's. Perhaps the postwar writers felt that all the worthwhile experimentation had already been done by their predecessors. The trend toward moderation continued as, with the progress of Japan's reconstruction, the society came to provide a comfortable living for an increasingly large portion of its population. A greater number of citizens with no interest in theories began to write satirical poems in seventeen syllables and send them to newspapers and magazines. They knew nothing about symbolist senryu or proletarian senryu; they simply wrote 5-7-5 syllable poems whenever they encountered a noteworthy incident or learned about one through the mass media. When the U.S.-inspired curriculum was introduced in Japanese schools, they came up with senryu like:

sex education—	*sei kyōiku*
children look bored	*meshibe oshibe ni*
with pistils and stamens	*ko wa akiru*[27]

When industrialization began endangering the environment, they wrote such senryu as:

how like a deformed fish	*kikeigyo no*
the island chain of Japan	*katachi ni mieru*
looks on the map!	*Nihon chizu*[28]

When some corrupt politicians tried to escape criminal charges by placing the blame on their secretaries, one senryu writer mimicked their words:

That house of mine,	*ano ie wa*
my secretary built it	*hisho ga katte ni*
without my knowledge	*tatemashita*[29]

Another senryu writer, on hearing how the O. J. Simpson murder trial ended in Los Angeles, expressed her puzzlement:

[27] *By Michio. Quoted in Yomiuri Shinbunsha, ed.,* Jiji senryū hyakunen, *146.*

[28] *By Keinosuke. Quoted in ibid., 181.*

[29] *Written by Nakamura Bunzō and translated by Matthew Spellman. Bito Sanryu, ed.,* Senryū: Haiku Reflections of the Times, *14. Reprinted by permission of Mangajin Inc./ Wasabi Brothers and Sekai Shuppan, Ltd.*

Modern day L.A.	*gendai no*
also had its own version	*Rosu ni mo atta*
of Rashomon	*yabu no naka*[30]

Contributed by ordinary citizens to the mass media, these poems typify the large majority of senryu written in the second half of the twentieth century.

The last example cited above was composed by a woman. One notable phenomenon in the last several decades has been a marked increase in the number of women who write senryu. It is part of a new development in Japanese literature in general: with a washing machine, a vacuum cleaner, and an automobile in every household, married women have been freed from many of the time-consuming chores in and around the house, and some of them have begun using the saved time for creative writing. Their senryu often provide perspectives on life that had been missing before. Typical is a collection that came out in 1987 and sold more copies than any other book of senryu in modern times. Entitled *Yūfuren* (The Love of a Married Woman), the collection presents in a boldly sensual language various shades of amorous thought that float across a married woman's mind. To quote a couple of examples:

with a man	*osu de aru*
who is merely a male	*dake no otoko to*
I look beyond the sea	*mite iru oki*

a lovebite—	*aikō ya*

[30] *Written by Ishida Sachiko and translated by Matthew Spellman. Ibid., 114. Reprinted by permission of Mangajin Inc./ Wasabi Brothers and Sekai Shuppan, Ltd. Rashomon, a prize-winning film directed by Kurosawa Akira, depicts a murder trial in which various witnesses give such radically different accounts of the same incident that what actually happened is never known.*

in the far, far distance	*haruka kanata ni*
cherry blossoms fall	*sakura chiru*[31]

In these and other outstanding examples the author, Toki-zane Shinko (b. 1929), showed that senryu can indeed be love poetry—the type of poetry at which Japanese women have traditionally excelled.

As the public response to *Yūfuren* has shown, senryu continues to be popular in today's Japan in spite of the no-ticeable decline of interest in literature among general readers. According to the 1997 edition of *Senryū nenkan* (Senryu Yearbook), there are 680 groups of senryu writers with headquarters in various cities and towns throughout the country. In addition to journals published by many of these groups, most daily newspapers and many weekly magazines also provide senryu columns, to which tens of thousands of readers submit their verses. According to an article published in 1997, the Tokyo newspaper *Yomiuri* receives on the average one thousand senryu submissions each day. The chance of one's verse being accepted for publication in that newspaper is well under one percent. Senryu are broadcast on television, too. Japan Broadcast-ing Corporation was the first to launch a program called "Senryū tengoku" (Senryu Paradise); its first broadcast in 1983 attracted more than 25,000 verses. The Daiichi Sei-mei Insurance Company started a nationwide senryu contest in 1987, specifically seeking verses that dealt with the life of a *sarariiman* (salaried white-collar worker). The contest has been held each year since, and in 1994 the number of entries reached 78,985. Some leaders of sen-ryu organizations lament that there are only about fifty thousand people who regularly write senryu in today's Japan, while there are some five million haiku poets. They ignore the fact, however, that any literate person

[31] *Tokizane Shinko, Yūfuren, 88, 163. Reprinted by permission of Ms. Tokizane.*

can—and often does—write senryu, whereas most haiku
are composed by those with some knowledge and training
in that verse form. Senryu will continue to be written for
as long as human nature remains imperfect and human
society falls short of being a paradise. For our health's
sake, we have to laugh.

Light Verse
from the
Floating World

1. We Are Swordless, but Not Wordless

In eighteenth-century Japan samurai were at the top of the social hierarchy, ruling over peasants, artisans, and merchants. They enjoyed a number of special privileges, including the right to wear two swords and to cut down on the spot any commoner who they thought acted improperly toward them. The highest-ranking samurai was the shogun, the powerful generalissimo who controlled all the territorial barons, known as daimyo, and thereby reigned over the entire nation. Ordinary samurai lived on annual stipends of rice or on incomes from land given by the shogun or a daimyo. They were warriors by definition, but in peacetime they served as officials and administrators at all levels of government. Because the shogun's castle was located in Edo, and because all the daimyo were required to spend half their time residing there with selected vassals, Edo had a large samurai population: roughly one-half of the people who lived in Edo belonged to the warrior class. The other half consisted of artisans and merchants—or *chōnin* (townspeople) as they were collectively called—who were at the lower end of the social scale. Given the crowded condition of the city, tension had to grow between the samurai and the chōnin, especially after the latter became affluent due to the growth of the commercial economy.

Edo townsmen used senryu as a means of releasing that tension. They ridiculed all aspects of contemporary samurai life, but their favorite targets were two. One was the effort of samurai to keep a dignified appearance at all times, despite the fact that they too shared in such foibles of human nature as greed, lust, and vanity. Especially laughed at was their pretense of keeping up high moral standards and not minding material poverty. Whereas artisans and merchants enjoyed a steady income by adjusting to price fluctuations, samurai were defenseless against inflation as they lived on fixed incomes. The shogun as well as the daimyo, who had exhausted most of their financial resources by the end of the seventeenth century, were not able to help their samurai employees, though they implemented reforms a number of times during the eighteenth century. At times they even resorted to such desperate measures as the debasement of the coinage, but to no avail. All this while the government enforced sumptuary laws and tried to promote austerity as the foremost moral principle. Samurai themselves had no choice but to adhere to this kind of asceticism, since it was the very basis on which their high social status had been justified. To engage in business would have been to debase themselves to the level of the merchant class and so fall to the bottom of the social hierarchy.

The other conspicuous target of ridicule in the senryu that dealt with samurai life had to do with corruption in government bureaucracy. The golden years of senryu roughly coincided with the so-called Tanuma period (1760–1786), which was notorious for loose morals among officials of all ranks. The period was named after Tanuma Okitsugu (1719–1786), the shogun's personal adviser and the most powerful man in government, who reportedly justified bribery by arguing that a man's loyalty is effectively measured by the value of the gift he gives because it is the measure of his self-sacrifice. That report has not been authenticated, and many descriptions of Tanuma's moral character that survive today seem to have been distorted by the political rivals who succeeded him in office.

Still, there is no denying that bribery of officials did exist at that time as it would in almost any government.

Very likely it was practiced more openly under a pragmatic politician like Tanuma who aggressively implemented new economic measures than it would have been under an idealistic statesman who believed more in the social benefits of moral education. The government officials, most of whom belonged to the samurai class and were underpaid to a greater or a lesser degree, would have needed strong principles indeed to decline the gifts that some merchants were all too willing to give.

a bamboo spear—
cut its head off, and it's
still a spear[1]

gift after gift—
the official's sleeve pockets
showing wear and tear

[1] There were a number of civil uprisings in premodern Japan. The rebellious civilians, who were not allowed to own swords, used bamboo spears for weapons.

takeyari wa kiri otoshite mo moto no yari (SHM: Hōreki 9)

sode no shita tabi kasanarite hokorobiru (SHM: Meiwa 4)

if you forget a gift
for the samurai at the gate—
"Halt! Where're you going?"

when you put it
into his mouth, he can't say a word—
a gold coin

tsuketodoke senu to monban korya doko e (Y 18)

hōbaru to nani mo iwarenu no ga koban (Y 21)

inside a gift box
labeled WONDER DRUG
a gold coin

the official's little son—
how fast he's learned to open
and close his fist![1]

[1] One of the most famous senryu of all time. See the Introduction for further commentary.

myōyaku wo akereba naka wa koban nari (Y 1)

yakunin no ko wa niginigi wo yoku oboe (Y 1)

a gift of sea bream
officially noted:
"Uh-huh"[1]

it's always needed
when deputy officials meet—
a samisen[2]

[1] A sea bream is the most prized fish in Japan. But the official in this senryu, who is used to expensive gifts, does not even say thanks.
[2] A samisen is a guitarlike musical instrument used by professional entertainers.

tai gurai tada un un to goaisatsu (Y 8)

sōdan ni samisen no iru orusushû (SHM: An'ei 4)

ten percent
is for the cost of women:
a successful bid

to His Lordship's page
the short sword is a tool
for digging up worms[1]

WE ARE SWORDLESS BUT NOT WORDLESS

[1] Evidently His Lordship spent most of his time fishing.

baishoku wo ichiwari irete fuda ga ochi (Y 11)

wakizashi de mimizu hojikuru kozamurai (Y 160)

how pathetic!
under the staircase
His Lordship's page[1]

His Lordship's past:
a tramp who used to sleep
in the fields and hills[2]

[1] This senryu is a parody of a famous hokku Bashō wrote when he saw an old warrior's helmet displayed at a shrine:

how pathetic!	*muzan ya na*
under the helmet	*kabuto no shita no*
a cricket	*kirigirisu*

The page in the senryu is waiting for his master, who is spending time with a courtesan. Customarily a courtesan's room was located on the second floor.

[2] Many daimyo were descendants of local samurai who rose to high rank by taking advantage of the social chaos in late medieval Japan.

muzan ya na hashigo no shita no zōritori (YS 4)

daimyō no kako wa no ni fushi yama ni fushi (YS 10)

every year without fail
His Lordship must trim the horns
on a woman's head[1]

for Her Ladyship
married life is only
one-half as long

[1] Under the shogun's rule a daimyo was obligated to spend alternate years in Edo and in his fief. Normally his wife lived in Edo all the time, while he kept a concubine in his home province. The senryu suggests that each woman was as jealous as a she-devil (horned in popular belief) during the time when the daimyo was away from her.

daimyō wa ichinen oki ni tsuno wo mogi (Y 1)

okusama wa ni no dan de waru goisshō (Y 3)

artistically clueless—
Her Ladyship graduated
from the bathroom[1]

His Lordship's maid
often races along the hallway
puffing and blowing[2]

[1] Some daimyo's concubines were former chambermaids who helped them with the chores of daily life, such as taking a bath. Tokugawa Yoshimune, who reigned as shogun from 1716 to 1745, was known to have been born of such a concubine.
[2] The maid cannot scream, because her pursuer is the drunken lord.

bukiyō na mekake yudono no agari nari (SHM: An'ei 1)

koshimoto wa dodo goroka wo hitotsuiki (Y 6)

His Lordship's concubine
has a few close friends:
skivvies and housemaids

                              thanks to his sister
                              he's on a horse that's
                              teaching him to ride[1]

[1] Because his beautiful sister became his lord's concubine, the man was promoted to samurai rank and given a horse. Yet, lacking the proper samurai training, he does not know how to ride.

omekake no tomodachi ima ni hashita nari (Y 12)

imōto no okage de uma ni kabussari (Y 3)

he goes riding
wherever his horse goes—
the upstart samurai

His Lordship's concubine
is barren, so she gets
a husband[1]

[1] One of the purposes of a daimyo taking in a concubine was to ensure an heir to his fiefdom. If she failed to fulfill that expectation, he would marry her off to one of his retainers.

uma no yuku hō e notteku niwakabushi (Y 14)

omekake wa harami kojirete en ni tsuki (YS 2)

all he does at work:
count the number of hairs
in his lord's nostrils[1]

samurai's quarrel
doesn't end, until it produces
two widows[2]

[1] In peacetime an ordinary samurai had little work to do, though he went to his lord's mansion daily. "To count the number of hairs in one's nostrils" was a phrase that, in addition to what it literally meant, described a person fawning on his superior.
[2] According to the Way of the Warrior, conceding defeat was considered an act of cowardice. Thus when two samurai quarreled they often fought with their swords until one killed the other. The survivor would then commit suicide to avoid the shame of being investigated, or flee from home to avoid the pursuit of the victim's children, who would be keen on revenge. See the Introduction for additional commentary.

ohanage wo kazoete iru ga tsutome nari (Y 24)

mononofu no kenka ni goke ga futari deki (Y 4)

"Drunken samurai!"
at once, the blossom viewing
comes to an end

witness to
a murder in the street
the stone Buddha[1]

[1] Because samurai were allowed to carry swords all the time, inevitably there were some who abused the privilege when they thought no one else was watching.

samurai ga yotte hanami no kyō ga same (SHM: Meiwa 4)

tsujigiri wo mite owashimasu jizōson (Y 1)

proud samurai,
why do you come here, looking
like a merchant?[1]

what? a surrender?
the samurai is handing over
both of his swords

[1] Yoshiwara, the largest brothel district of Edo, was for the townsmen; it was not for the people of the warrior class, who were expected to maintain a high moral standard. When a samurai visited there he had to disguise himself or, at least, hand over his swords at the entrance to the district.

hito wa bushi naze chōnin ni natte kuru (Y 5)

kōsan no yō ni daishō watasu nari (Y 18)

the samurai asks her
as soon as he's seated:
"What time is it?"[1]

as if it were
a military art, they talk
of austerity[2]

[1] While a townsman was able to stay in Yoshiwara all night, an employed samurai had to return to his barracks by curfew, which was usually at six P.M.
[2] The shogunate formerly promoted military arts among samurai, but many years of peace had rendered such promotion meaningless. Now the government had no option but to advocate austerity as the foremost moral principle, because many samurai received subsistence-level salaries.

samurai wa suwaru to sugu ni toki wo kiki (YS 6)

ken'yaku wo bugei no yō ni iitateru (Y 7)

like fruits
bird cages grow on trees
around the barracks[1]

"My wife isn't sociable"
says the samurai, hiding
his lack of something[2]

[1] Low-ranking samurai were housed in barracks. Not able to live on their salaries alone, some of them bred pet birds to earn extra money.
[2] It seems that his wife's better clothes are all at the pawnshop.

torikago no ki ni natte iru kumi yashiki (Y 23)

goshinzo no degirai jitsu wa kore ga nashi (Y 24)

life of austerity:
the nanny he's hired
doubles as a concubine

the samurai too
wants to get a high price
for the rice he sells[1]

[1] Usually samurai received their stipends in rice. They had to sell it whenever they needed cash.

ken'yaku de uba wa mekake to futayaku shi (SHM: Meiwa 4)

mononofu mo kome wo ba takaku uritagari (SHM: Hōreki 11)

when he takes off
his samurai gear, his talk
turns sly

a last resort:
the samurai puts his soul
in pawn[1]

[1] According to the Way of the Warrior, a samurai was to treasure his sword as if it were his soul. See the Introduction for additional commentary.

kamishimo wo nugu to kotoba mo zuruku nari (K 5)

tamashii wo seppa zumatte shichi ni oki (Y 39)

"A splendid sword!"
says the pawnbroker
tossing a pittance

looks like a townsman
when he leaves the pawnshop—
how pathetic!

kore wa gomeisaku to bantō hyaku nage (Y 18)

chōnin de shichiya wo deru wa hidoi koto (Y 10)

2. The Mad, Mad World of Work

Edo townsmen earned their livelihood by pursuing a wide variety of occupations. *Kinsei shokunin zukushi ekotoba* (Picture Scrolls of Modern Artisans), completed by Kuwagata Keisai (1764–1824) in 1805, humorously depicts urban workmen engaged in more than one hundred different trades that range from carpentry and roofing to selling eels and staging a monkey show. Many such occupations stayed within the family through generations, the father upon his retirement handing his trade over to his eldest son or the most qualified one. Other male children were sent out to learn other trades or trained at home until they were ready to become independent. In most specialized pursuits, boys had to start a rigorous training program in their early teens and spend many years of in-house apprenticeship before they were publicly recognized as professionals. Inevitably, people with the same speciality came to share certain behavioral and personality traits, providing good subject matter for senryu writers.

Of the occupations ridiculed in premodern senryu, three distinctly stand out. The first is the medical profession. Physicians became a favorite target of senryu writers probably because there was an abundance of unqualified doctors whose treatments seemed ineffective. Since no license was needed to become a physician, and since the profession guaranteed a good income, people of all social classes called themselves doctors and practiced medicine with little or no training. A five-volume directory of physicians published in 1819–20 lists the names of some 2,500 doctors taking patients in Edo. No doubt some of them were competent physicians who had a good knowledge of Chinese medicine, Dutch medicine, or both. Yet, with no government mechanism for quality control, there must have been a number of self-appointed physicians who deserved the name of *yabuisha* (quack doctor), as senryu writers contemptuously called them.

Harshly criticized also were Buddhist priests. Part of the reason was the diminished role of religion in the spiritual life of Edo townsmen, but it also had something to do with the low morale of the priesthood in general. The shogunate, remembering how strongly monks had resisted government control in the sixteenth century, subsequently implemented a series of measures to curtail their extrareligious activities, in exchange guaranteeing a high social status and steady income. Completely integrated into the feudal system, many priests became mere functionaries who performed religious ceremonies on appropriate occasions. The comfortable temple life soon led to the moral degradation of some priests, giving rise to the kind of shameful conduct lampooned in senryu.

The third group of people who were frequently made fun of in senryu occupied a much lower place in society. They were maidservants who came to Edo from the neighboring rural provinces and who did household chores for the more affluent townspeople. Although the work was hard and the pay was low, young daughters of impoverished peasants were all too willing to move to the city and taste the higher standard of living. A report compiled in 1843 indicates that the number of migrant female workers in Edo was 8,353. The figure must have been considerably larger before 1788, when the government issued an ordinance requiring an official work permit for any outsider to come and work in the city. By all indications these girls were good-natured, hard workers, but in comparison with city-bred women they were noticeably less refined in appearance, language, and deportment. They were precisely the kind of people who elicited a feeling of superiority in the minds of senryu writers.

the doctor has a cold
but he's eating noodle soup
and resting in bed[1]

"Something you shouldn't do . . . "
he pauses, since his patient's
young wife is close by[2]

[1] The doctor knows his own prescriptions are useless.
[2] It seems that a doctor on house call is talking to his patient, who has a beautiful wife.

ishadono wa kekku udon de hikkaburi (YS 9)

dokudate ni hana no saki no wa iinikushi (Y 5)

His Lordship's doctor—
in his hand, even orange peel
does not look cheap[1]

"There'll soon be
a charming widow"—that's the talk
among the doctors

[1] Orange peel was a common ingredient in traditional Chinese medicine.

gotenyaku chinpi mo yasuku mienu nari (Y 5)

yoi goke ga dekiru to hanasu isha nakama (Y 5)

unmatched
in the art of matchmaking—
the doctor[1]

just the right number
of yawns in the waiting room—
good medical practice[2]

[1] A practicing physician usually has a wide circle of acquaintances. He is also a smooth talker. Thus he often doubles as a marriage broker.
[2] If the waiting room is empty, a patient may suspect the doctor's reputation. But if the room is too crowded and the patient had to wait long, he may get irritated.

nakōdo ni kakete wa shigoku meii nari (Y 13)

genkan de akubi wo saseru sajikagen (Y 4)

"Sudden change for the worse"
a doctor always has
that escape clause

the doctors
praise his deathbed poem
then hurry to leave

hen to iu nigemichi isha wa akete oku (Y 23)

ishashū wa jisei wo homete tatarekeri (Y 2)

sending his colleague
just in time for the last rite —
good medical practice

how quackish
he looks! the doctor at his
patient's funeral

todome wo ba yojin ni saseru sajikagen (Y 24)

heta sōna isha sōrei e mieru nari (Y 13)

the doctor gets paid
by the victim he's killed—
great business to be in!

the quack doctor
while curing one patient
lets two others expire

koroshita wo yokoseba yabui yoi shigoto (Y 24)

yabuisha wa hitori ikasu to futari shini (Y 18)

when the quack doctor
arrives, a smell of death
wafts into the house

a sudden shower—
at the quack's gate
a crowd gathers[1]

[1] What the crowd seeks is not the doctor's treatment but shelter from the rain. It seems that the doctor has an imposing house with a large, roofed gate.

yabuisha no haitta ie ni sakki tachi (Y 13)

niwakaame yabui no kado no nigiyakasa (Y 18)

the Zen monk
done with his meditation
looks for fleas[1]

since he buys it
from the grocer, nobody
in his parish knows[2]

THE MAD, MAD WORLD OF WORK

[1] See the Introduction for commentary on this verse.
[2] What he buys is a fish, which a Buddhist priest is prohibited from eating. Buying it from a fishmonger would be too conspicuous.

Zenshū wa zazen ga sumu to nomi wo tori (Y 2)

yaoya kara uru to wa zoku no shiranu koto (Y 5)

after the cardinal's robe
became his to wear, he thinks more
of the floating world

when the priest goes
to a brothel in his parish
he wears his robe[1]

[1] When the priest goes to a brothel in his parish, it is to perform some kind of religious service. When he wants to buy a prostitute, he will disguise himself and go to a brothel outside his parish.

hi no koromo kireba ukiyo ga oshiku nari (Y 1)

jorōya e koromo de kuru wa dannadera (Y 26)

"Put on your disguise
at the riverside inn"
thus spake the Master[1]

whenever a priest
enters a riverside inn
a doctor comes out[2]

[1] "Thus spake the Master" mimicks the tone of a Confucian classic. In this senryu, the master is an aged priest teaching a young acolyte how to disguise himself when going to Yoshiwara.
[2] The disguise a priest most commonly used when he went to Yoshiwara was that of a physician.

funayado de bakeyare to shi notamawaku (Y 3)

nakayado e shukke hairu to isha ga deru (Y 19)

the priest earns
all that money, and the doctor
fritters it away

little by little
his sermon draws the widow
into a strange faith

shukke de mōketa wo isha de tsukai sute (Y 19)

sorosoro to goke wo jahō e susumekomi (Y 12)

leaving the priest's quarters
with a shocked expression
a respectable widow

"There is no hell"—
to his mistress, the priest
tells the truth

kyōzamegao de kuri wo deru katai goke (Y 21)

kakoware ni jigoku wa nai to jitsu wo ii (Y 4)

"Don't ever come
near my living room"
the priest reminds her[1]

what a fancy service!
no wonder, the priest did it
for his mistress's mother

[1] The priest seems to be talking to his secret mistress, who is living at his temple.

kanarazu kuri e deyaruna to oshō ii (Y 17)

kakoware no haha nengoro ni ekō sare (Y 24)

the maid's letter
as if written in some warped
Sanskrit characters

after a scolding
the maid serves up
like a thunderclap

gejo no fumi bonji wo hineru yō ni kaki (Y 2)

shikarareta gejo zendate no nigiyakasa (Y 34)

the young master
who scolds the maid in the daytime
worships her at night

the maid
who follows his orders at night
doesn't during the day

wakadanna yoru wa ogande hiru shikari (SHM: Meiwa 3)

iu koto wo yoru kiku gejo wa hiru kikazu (Y 51)

sticking up two fingers
on her forehead like horns
the maid skedaddles[1]

each time she's laughed at
the maid shakes a few hayseeds
from her hair

.

[1] The maid is mimicking a jealous she-devil, which her mistress would turn into if she
were to acquiesce to her master's wishes.

yubi nihon hitai e atete gejo wa nige (Y 3)

warawareru tabi ni inaka no aka ga nuke (Y 8)

after reading it
the maidservant says
"I hate Senryū"

the laundryman
feeds on the filth
of his neighbors

gejo yonde mite Senryū wa nikui yatsu (Y 91)

sentakuya kinjo no hito no aka de kui (Y 36)

at each corner
the tatami maker swears
at the carpenter[1]

"Swords drawn!"—
the ladder salesman flees
to the nearest roof

[1] *Tatami* are thick straw mats of uniform dimensions, about three feet by six feet. A traditional Japanese house is built so that the size of each room will be suitable for laying out a certain number of tatami, usually six or eight.

sumizumi de daiku wo soshiru tatamisashi (Y 26)

hashigouri nukimi to kiite yane e nige (Y 2)

the chinaware seller—
when his business crashes
the whole neighborhood knows[1]

rocks at the corner
finally breathing with life
the gardener takes a puff[2]

[1] A merchant usually wants to hide his losses, but the sound of breaking chinaware is unmistakable.
[2] A well-known teaching in landscape gardening is: "Make everything in the garden look as if it were breathing with life."

setomonoya atari kinjo e son ga shire (Y 5)

sumi no ishi yōyō ikite suitsukeru (Y 17)

the storyteller
lets the villain in his tale
escape—to tomorrow[1]

the lion dancer
when his show is finished
chokes the lion to death

[1] A professional storyteller often narrated parts of a long story day by day.

kōshaku no teki wa ashita e nigenobite (YS 6)

daikagura shimau to shishi wo shime koroshi (Y 14)

the ladle seller
serves portions of air
to display his wares

when the debate
is about room rent, he loses out—
the Confucian scholar

hishaku uri nan ni mo nai wo kunde mise (Y 4)

tanachin de iikomerareru rongoyomi (Y 5)

no danger whatever
yet up rushes the boatman
to hold her stepping down

if the ferryman
is too kind-hearted
his boat may sink[1]

[1] A good-natured ferryman finds it hard to refuse passengers even when his boat is already overloaded. This senryu may be intended to be read as a maxim on leadership.

abunaku mo nai ni sendō dakitagari (Y 49)

kokoroyoku noseru to watashi shizumu nari (SHM: Meiwa 7)

the chef
while he sharpens his knife
leaves the carp swimming[1]

somehow the palmist
always finds a line
that is not good

[1] See the Introduction for commentary.

ryōrinin togu uchi koi wo oyogaseru (Y 3)

te no suji wo miru to hitosuji kechi wo tsuke (Y 2)

the sumo wrestler—
a crowd of fans swarming
below his chest

when he holds a baby
his entire body shrinks—
the sumo wrestler

sekitori no chichi no atari ni hitodakari (Y 1)

ko wo daite sōmi no sukumu sumōtori (Y 6)

"Lock up the doors
when you go to bed," says the thief
leaving for work

finding someone at home
the burglar asks, "Excuse me,
which is the way to . . . ?"

yoku shimete nero to ii ii nusumi ni de (YS 10)

hito ga ite hirudorobō wa michi wo kiki (Yanagikori 3)

when he hears a snore
the masseur lets his hands
fall asleep too

professional smile
of the mortician's wife:
a look of grief[1]

---

[1] See the Introduction for commentary.

anmatori ibiki wo kiku to tenuki wo shi (Y 2)

aisō ni koshiya no naigi beso wo kaki (YS 3)

3. Love in Chains

Love either before or outside marriage was severely repressed in eighteenth-century Japan, because all unbridled passions were thought to pose a potential danger to the order of feudal society. Buddhism equated love with lust, and Confucianism also considered it incompatible with the highest principles of duty to the state. Thus in the samurai class a love affair was a crime punishable by death. Although commoners took a more lenient attitude, they still preferred to see their unmarried sons and daughters refrain from any romantic involvements and in due time accept a match arranged in view of social, familial, and business circumstances. Predictably, the contemporary codes of conduct were stricter for girls, demanding that they not act in any way that might be construed as provocative. In actuality, however, such codes often proved ineffective in preventing the natural manifestations of a human instinct, and most parents were realistic enough to admit that. When the codes were broken, the families of the young culprits in many cases showed understanding toward them and handled the situation in a reasonable way. The most stubborn obstacle was usually the father because he had to think of the family honor, but eventually he would accede to the tearful pleading of the mother and give his blessing.

In cases where the young couple was not given the traditional blessing, tragedies sometimes occurred in the form of double suicide. Such suicide took place more frequently in the late seventeenth century, after popular writ-

ers like Ihara Saikaku (1642–1693) and Chikamatsu Monzaemon (1653–1724) had glorified it in their works. To be
sure, many of those who committed love suicide were
married men and their favorite courtesans, but their manner of death suggested what young lovers could do if they
saw no other alternative. Alarmed, many local govern-
ments issued ordinances prohibiting love suicide; in Edo,
those who attempted it and failed were arrested and exposed to public view for three days in the busiest part of
the city. Failed suicide attempts were not uncommon,
since many of those who wanted to kill themselves
jumped into a river or a canal or a well at night, without
realizing there were passersby.

Most young townspeople were less daring, however,
and they were willing to accept a marriage arranged by
their families. Consequently, there were instances of the
bride and the groom meeting for the first time at their
wedding ceremony. But in most cases the go-between
would set up a *miai*, an introductory meeting between the
two families, at a restaurant or a theater or a seasonal festival before any serious marriage talk began. Such a brief
meeting hardly gave a chance for the young couple to get
to know each other, but at least each was able to find out
how the other looked. After the miai the families mulled
over their impressions of each other and decided whether
they would pursue the matter further. If the decision was
positive on both sides, the matchmaker went ahead and
arranged a formal engagement.

The go-between who set up such marriages was usually
someone who by profession had a wide circle of acquaintances — a physician, a music teacher, a landlord who
owned a tenement house, or a businessman who operated
a large store. He or she had to be a smooth talker and skillful negotiator, since the families involved would express all
kinds of concern over the postmarital life of their sons and
daughters. The matchmaker had to spend a good deal of
time talking to the two families and convincing them how

perfect the match would be. The reward for these efforts could be handsome—usually ten percent of the bride's dowry—when the nuptial knot was successfully tied. It was no wonder that some go-betweens became overeager to bring couples together, thereby providing good material for senryu writers.

just by showing
her bare skin, a woman
becomes a felon

she can't read
he can't write, yet between them
a romance

hadaka mi wo miseru mo onna tsumi ni nari (Y 15)

yoman doshi kakan dōshi no koi mo koi (YS 3)

where there's a will
the eyes can speak as much
as the mouth

first eye to eye
then hand to hand
and mouth to mouth

ki ga areba me mo kuchi hodo ni mono wo ii (YS 2)

mazu me to me sore kara te to te kuchi to kuchi (Y 102)

the woman, after
making sure she looks decent,
tosses a coin[1]

a woman's sleeve:
what a fine curtain for her tongue
when it slips!

[1] A scene at a shrine. A woman in public view has to be careful when she takes some physical action, because the kimono she wears is a loose-fitting garment not intended for lively movements. She also knows that feminine charm is best displayed when she does take such an action.

sansen wo migoshirae shite onna nage (Y 16)

furisode wa iisokonai no futa ni nari (Y 1)

a charming gesture—
the girl knows it, as she covers
her mouth with her sleeve

to make herself look good
she's given the maid a hairdo
as fancy as her own[1]

[1] A scene of a well-dressed woman going out. In her thinking, even the maidservant accompanying her is an adornment that adds to her appearance.

aisō ni musume wa kuchi e sode wo ate (Y 9)

mi no date ni gejo ga kami made yutte yari (Y 1)

when a baby
is in her arms, it's easier
to talk to a man[1]

the love letter
from a man she doesn't care for—
she shows it to mother

[1] With a baby in her arms, she can rest assured that the man won't dare do anything improper. She also knows the baby does not understand their conversation. The baby is probably her sister's or a neighbor's.

ko wo dakeba otoko ni mono ga iiyasushi (Y 1)

waga sukanu otoko no fumi wa haha ni mise (Y 4)

"I love you"
such brief words, yet how hard
to say them!

to put it briefly
courting is tantamount
to begging

horeta to wa mijikai koto no iinikusa (Mutamagawa 1)

temijika ni ieba kudoki mo mushin nari (YS 6)

"I love you"—
if a woman says that
she's really desperate[1]

she remembers
the date of their last meeting—
now there's a woman!

[1] A man was expected to take the initiative in matters of love, especially so in feudal times when reserve was considered one of the foremost virtues for women.

horeta to wa onna no yabure kabure nari (Y 4)

ōta hi wo oboete iru ga onna no ki (Y 2)

"Will you stop, please?"
when she says it in a *low* voice
I may get lucky

how long it seems
when you unwind a woman's sash
while lying in bed!

yoshinā no hikui wa sukoshi dekikakari (Y 1)

nete tokeba obi hodo nagaki mono wa nashi (Y 3)

the clerk and the maid
are not on speaking terms—
in the daytime, that is

she has no artistic
skills, because of what her
big sister has done[1]

[1] Girls had few opportunities to go out, far less to socialize. Taking a music lesson was one such rare opportunity. Apparently the older sister in this senryu took advantage of the opportunity and did something that upset her parents.

sono tedai sono gejo hiru wa mono iwazu (Y 1)

imōto no mugei wa ane no furachi yue (Y 6)

she is a girl
who can't be married to someone
who knows about her

"Older daughter first"
the parents kept saying, until
the younger eloped

shitta hō e wa agerarenu musume nari (Y 19)

ane kara to itteru uchi ni imoto nige (Y 34)

the abducted girl —
so often that night, she was seen
going out the back door

with no more ado
she confesses the truth
in the fifth month

katsugareru yoi ni shige shige ura e deru (Y 7)

massugu ni hakujō wo suru itsutsukime (Y 9)

threatened with a well
and a rope, her parents agree
to take him in[1]

love suicide—
the fishmonger's account
has fins and tails[2]

[1] "If you don't approve our marriage, I'll either drown or hang myself," the daughter had
said to her parents.
[2] Many of those who committed love suicide threw themselves into a river. Witnesses were
often fish vendors living on the banks. A Japanese idiom for dramatizing a story is *ohire wo
tsuku*, or "to add fins and tails."

oyatachi wa ido to kubi to de muko wo tori (Y 4)

shinjū wo sakanaya ohire wo tsukete ii (Y 9)

"You can have the baby"
they tell the girl on the bridge
and bring her home

united at last
in death, a pair
of happy faces

harande mo ii to hashi kara tsurete kuru (Y 21)

shinikitte ureshisō naru kao futatsu (Y 1)

four people
grieve, because of
two afraid[1]

the matchmaker
speaks the sober truth
only when drunk

[1] A riddle-like senryu. The "four people" must be the parents of the "two," who have committed love suicide.

yottari no nageki ki no chiisana futari (Y 11)

nakōdo wa yōte iu no ga hon no koto (YS 1)

often killed off
by the matchmaker: a future
sister-in-law[1]

"Just a father-in-law
whose days are numbered"
says the matchmaker[2]

[1] It was hard enough for the new bride to deal with her mother-in-law. The hardship
would multiply if her husband had sisters living in the same house. A matchmaker trying
to arrange a marriage would reduce the number of the prospective bride's future sisters-in-
law by at least one.
[2] According to the matchmaker, this would be an ideal marriage for the bride because the
groom's mother is dead and his father is virtually dead.

nakōdo wa kojūto hitori korosu nari (Y 4)

kage no nai shūto hitori to nakodo ii (Y 18)

the go-between
even praised the rain
before taking his leave

meet by chance
then by appointment—
the modern way

nakōdo wa ame made homete kaeru nari (YS 1)

arakajime mite kara yobu ga ima no fū (SHM: Meiwa 3)

so that the two
may pass each other on the road
the matchmaker schemes

the engaged couple:
they catch the same cold, one
after the other

surichigau yō ni nakōdo kumen wo shi (YS 1)

iinazuke tagai chigai ni kaze wo hiki (Y 1)

engaged
she feels like a houseguest
in her own home

"I don't love him
but I don't hate him," she says
of her fiancé[1]

[1] In an arranged marriage, the couple hardly had a chance to get to know each other
before the wedding.

yuinō ga kuru to musume mo kakaribito (SHM: Meiwa 1)

kāiku mo nikuku mo nai to iinazuke (SHM: An'ei 4)

to the go-between
"Delay it four or five days"
she says in a low voice[1]

if it's your parents
you heed when you marry
the bride would be past it[2]

[1] It was the go-between's job to set a date for the wedding. Here the bride-to-be does not give the reason why she wants the wedding to be postponed, but from her low voice and the words "four or five days" the go-between immediately guesses what it is.
[2] A young woman is inexperienced as a homemaker. A filial son who really wants to help his parents by marrying would look for an older woman.

nakōdo e shigonichi nobasu hikui koe (Y 1)

kōkō ni motsu nyōbō wa toshi ga take (Y 2)

4. The Battle of the Sexes

The life of a married couple in premodern Japan operated on patriarchal principles that permeated the society. The husband was the head of family who managed its estate and who made all the important decisions on domestic matters. The wife was to follow his orders obediently, without raising any questions. *Onna daigaku* (The Great Learning for Women), a book published in 1780 to teach morality to young women, says: "A woman has no other lord. Think of your husband as the lord and serve him respectfully and judiciously." Unless the family was rich enough to hire a maid, the wife did all the household chores—cooking, cleaning, laundry, sewing, bringing up the children. The senryu

whenever the wife	*onaigi ga*
stands up, a sound of scissors	*tatsu to hasami no*
falling to the floor	*otsuru oto (Y 15)*

indicates that the wife had to do sewing even at those rare times when she was able to sit down. If she was a merchant's wife, she also helped to mind the store, in addition to all the housework.

Precisely because of the dominant position given to men in married life, writers of senryu were fond of making fun of henpecked husbands. Many of the husbands who appear in their verses are weak-willed, clumsy, and gullible. Especially laughed at was an *irimuko* (adopted husband), a man who married into his wife's family and lived in her parents' home. He had to be respectful of his wife because, even though he was the head of the family, all the other household members were related to her by blood and usually took her side when there was a difference of opinion. Often his father-in-law was the owner of the store where he worked, in which case his position was even weaker.

Another favorite subject of senryu dealing with domestic life was the cuckold, again because of the power and dignity associated with the husband's position at home. Whereas the wife had to endure her husband's divagations silently, the husband had the law entirely on his side to punish his partner if she was unfaithful. A samurai who caught his adulterous wife in the act was allowed to draw his sword and execute her on the spot. Townsmen liked to resolve the situation in less drastic ways. Their common practice was to cut the guilty wife's hair and oust her from the home. Sometimes the paramour paid money—usually five ryō (gold coins)—to the husband and settled the matter privately, as in:

with eyes glaring	*nyōbō wo*
at his wife, he receives	*nirande teishu*
five gold coins	*goryō tori (SHM: Meiwa 7)*

The husband can only glare at his wife, since he has no way to squeeze money out of her.

The cuckolded husband could chase his wife out of the home, however. Indeed, the prerogatives of a husband included the right to divorce his wife at any time and for any conceivable reason. All he had to do was write a brief letter declaring his decision to terminate the marriage. The wife had no recourse, no matter how unreasonable the decision might seem to her. Nor did she have any way of initiating a divorce procedure by herself, even when she had ample grounds on which to demand one. She might run away and take refuge in her parents' home, but without the letter of divorce from her husband she had to remain legally married to him for the rest of her life. The wife's only way out was to flee into a convent and take Buddhist vows. When she had spent three years of service as a nun, her husband was obligated to write her a letter of divorce.

The Buddhist convent best known to Edo townspeople in this connection was located at Tōkei Temple in Kamakura, some thirty miles southwest of the city. It is estimated that over two thousand married women fled there during the eighteenth century and the first half of the nineteenth century. According to senryu writers, a number of those who took temporary refuge were unfaithful wives who wanted a divorce so as to marry their paramours, but there is little historical evidence to confirm that supposition.

the one hundred gold coins
interest no one, since they bring
a certain bride

the one hundred gold coins
she brought are gone, yet her face
still remains

musume ga tsuku de moraite nashi hyakuryō (Y 24)

hyakuryō wa nakunari kao wa nokotteru (Y 23)

protecting the couple
from autumn winds, a gold screen
the bride has brought[1]

how beautiful
she looks—a bride
with nothing on[2]

[1] In the Japanese literary tradition an autumn wind symbolizes some destructive force, natural or man-made. The large dowry the bride has brought helps to keep domestic peace, regardless of her personal shortcomings.
[2] As explained in the Introduction, "a bride with nothing on" means a bride who brings no dowry. A beautiful girl needs no dowry to get married.

akikaze wo fusegu jisan no kinbyōbu (YS 1)

rippa naru mono hanayome no maruhadaka (Y 10)

courtesy calls by the bride:
menfolk see nothing
except her face[1]

not a word
she spoke, yet the house
has become the wife's[2]

[1] On the day of her wedding, a bride made courtesy calls on her new neighbors. The
neighborhood women would take the chance to scrutinize her from head to toe, apprais-
ing every little item that adorned her.
[2] See the Introduction for commentary.

yome no rei otoko no miru wa kao bakari (Y 21)

ichigon mo iwazu nyōbo no uchi ni nari (YS 18)

the beautiful wife
boiling his herb medicine
that doesn't work[1]

it nullifies
all the treatments by the doctor—
his wife's beauty[2]

[1] Very likely the medicine is an aphrodisiac.
[2] Despite the doctor's order, the husband does not allow himself a restful night's sleep.

ii nyōbo kikanu kusuri wo senjiteru (Y 21)

mudabone wo isha ni oraseru utsukushisa (SHM: Hōreki 13)

his wife
not being a tidy dresser
the store thrives

his wife away from home
he spends the entire day
looking for things

izumai no warui naigi de ureru mise (YS 3)

nyōbō ga rusu de ichinichi sagashigoto (K 5)

somewhere on earth
she'd tucked away what it took
to buy a silk sash

when he starts to look
for the sewing box, his wife
comes jumping out[1]

---

[1] For a married woman, her sewing box was the best place to hide money or anything else she didn't want her husband to know about.

dokkara ka dashite nyōbo wa obi wo kai (Y 5)

haribako wo sagasu to nyōbo tonde deru (Y 12)

his wife
badmouthes those who share
his taste in poetry[1]

after consulting
his wife, he becomes less
than a loyal friend[2]

[1] Forced to be realists by the material necessities of life, few housewives showed interest
in poetry. Also, the men who wrote poetry were often libertines who frequented the
pleasure quarters.
[2] It seems that the husband has been invited by his friends to go out for fishing or
blossom viewing or some such recreational activity. But his wife refuses to let him go
either because of the expense or because of her fear that the friends would take him to
the pleasure quarters on the way back.

nyōbō wa fūgetsu no tomo wo waruku ii (Y 14)

nyōbō to sōdan wo shite giri wo kaki (Y 1)

when a man
is afraid of his wife
the money piles up

after paying
the palanquin bearers
his wife sulks[1]

[1] The husband had to hire a palanquin to come home after he got drunk late at night.

nyōbō wo kowagaru yatsu wa kane ga deki (Y 3)

kagochin wo yatte nyōbo wa tsun to suru (Y 1)

the morning after
his wife plays it back
for him to hear[1]

no nagging on the day
her husband was a winner—
now there's a woman!

[1] There were no tape recorders in premodern Japan. In this senryu, it is the wife who
mimics the drunken husband's ravings of the night before.

akuru asa nyōbo wa kuda wo makimodoshi (Y 17)

katta hi wa iken iwanu ga onna nari (Y 7)

her husband's
becoming a little too kind
weighs on her mind

many excuses
he has used before — his wife
remembers them all

ingin ni natta otto ga ki ni kakari (Mutamagawa 4)

iinuke wo minna nyōbo ni oboerare (Y 10)

convenient
and inconvenient—
having a wife

for a housemaid
she's hired an old woman—
a nice surprise for him!

chōhō na mono no jama na wa nyōbo nari (YS 6)

meshitaki ni babā wo oite hana akase (Y 1)

the wife
on winning the argument
gets slapped in the face

having lashed out
too much at his wife
he's cooking the rice

ri ni katte nyōbo aenaku kurawasare (Y 14)

nyōbō wo shikari sugoshite meshi wo taki (YS 9)

for two days
his wife remains in bed
to get back at him

"Stop fussing
and just write the letter," says
the scornful wife[1]

[1] "The letter" is a letter of divorce. The wife knows her husband lacks the courage to divorce her.

futsuka nete nyōbo ikon wo harasu nari (Y 8)

sappari to kaite kure na to mikubirare (Y 4)

"You're divorced!"—
but his wife, who's heard it before,
just sits there, smoking

quarreling with him
all the time, she has become
big with their child

dete yuke ni narete nyōbo wa sutte iru (SHM: Hōreki 10)

isakai wo shii shii hara wo ōkiku shi (YS 3)

a childless wife can be
divorced, but how about the one
who bears too many?[1]

suckling the baby
in bed, she shakes her head
at her husband

[1] If a woman did not become pregnant after three years of married life, it was sufficient grounds for divorce.

ko no naki wa sarubeshi dekiru ni mo komari (Y 124)

soeji shite nani ka teishu ni kaburi furi (Y 2)

baby at her breast
she tells him, "There're sardines
on the shelf"

since their baby was born
telling him what to do
has become her habit

soeji shite tana ni iwashi ga gozarimasu (Y 14)

san ageku otto tsukau ga kuse ni nari (Y 3)

tonight the mother
is mad as hell, so the baby
sleeps in the middle

their hands touch
then their feet—in no time
an armistice

hara no tatsu ban mannaka e ko wo nekashi (SHM: Tenmei 6)

te ga sawari ashi ga sawatte nakanaori (Y 75)

the quarrel over
she sounds just like
a woman again

the quarrel over
she looks into the mirror:
now there's a woman!

nakanaori suru to onna no koe ni nari (Y 19)

nakanaori kagami wo miru wa onna nari (Y 4)

the measure
of her hate: she's left home
without the children

weapon of the wife
with no parent to go back to:
a well[1]

[1] A wife whose parents were dead had no place to take refuge when she had a fight with
her husband. She had no choice but to throw herself into a well—or, at least, such was
her threat when they fought.

nikushimi no tsuyosa kodomo wo oite nige (Y 12)

sato no nai nyōbo wa ido de kowagarase (Y 2)

"She hasn't come here!"—
a panic breaks out
at her parents' home

for Kamakura
she leaves, after standing awhile
on the river's edge[1]

[1] It took determination for a woman to become a nun, even for a three-year period. In this senryu, the woman has thought of throwing herself into a river before leaving for Tōkei Temple in Kamakura.

kotchi e wa konu to sato kara sawagidashi (Y 17)

Kamakura e yuku mae kawa e sude no koto (Y 14)

he wrote a letter
of divorce, then was kicked out—
the adopted husband

"She's my wife," he thinks—
that's where the adopted husband
fails to see the truth

sarijō wo kaku to irimuko ondasare (Y 10)

nyōbo da to omou ga muko no fukaku nari (Y 4)

"I'm just a servant
with a better-sounding name," thinks
the adopted husband

"That frightened of her?"
they let the adopted husband
go home at last

gaibun no yoi hōkō to muko omoi (Y 10)

sō kowai mono ka to muko wo kaesu nari (SHM: An'ei 4)

like a clothes thief
fleeing from a bathhouse —
the paramour

the newborn
won't look like the father —
the mother's secret

maotoko wa yuya nusubito no yō ni nige (SHM: Meiwa 4)

teteoya ni ninu wo shitta wa haha bakari (SHM: Meiwa 1)

the whole town
knows of it, except
the husband

he sought out
her paramour, and the scandal
grew bigger

chōnai de shiranu wa teishu bakari nari (S 4)

maotoko wo midashite haji wo ōkiku shi (Y 1)

a son is kicked out—
several houses down the street
a wife is divorced

she's been let go
yet in her mother's words
"She's left him"

kandō no shigoken saki de tsuma wo sari (Y 11)

dasareta wo detekita ni suru sato no haha (Y 8)

tailing the wife
until she reaches the border
her paramour[1]

a distraught woman
rambles here and there, all over
the Five Mountains[2]

[1] The border is that of the city of Edo. The woman, having slipped out of her home at night, hurries on her way to Tōkei Temple in Kamakura. Her worried paramour, for whose sake she wants a divorce, shadows her to the city limits, beyond which the arms of the municipal law do not reach.
[2] The Five Mountains refers to the five famous Zen temples in Kamakura. Because there are so many temples in Kamakura, it is not easy for a first-time visitor to find Tōkei Temple, which is not one of the five.

jifuku wo matagu made mippu mie kakure (Yanaibako 4)

urotaeta onna gozan wo atchi kochi (Y 13)

a distraught woman
rushes in, only to find
it's Kenchō Temple[1]

before the three years
are gone, her paramour has had
a change of heart

---

[1] Kenchō Temple, a famous Zen temple, was located near Tōkei Temple.

urotaeta kakekomi mo aru Kenchōji (SHM: Meiwa 3)

sannen no uchi ni maotoko ki ga kawari (Yanaibako 2)

might this change
his mind? she's caught smallpox
in Kamakura[1]

when he finally
falls in love with his wife
the end is near[2]

[1] Smallpox usually leaves ugly pockmarks on one's face.
[2] In an arranged marriage it sometimes took a long time for the couple to get to know each other.

ki ga kawarumai mono ka Kamakura de hōsō (Yanaibako 2)

nyōbō ni horeru to saki ga chikaku nari (Y 23)

5. Dimpled Little Lunatics

Children were treasured in premodern Japan. For one thing, their mortality rate was very high (out of every ten babies born, only five or six reached the age of sixteen), making the survivors so much more precious. For another, they were thought, because of their innocence, to be capable of communicating with deities; there were even sayings like "A child before the age of seven should be counted among the gods." More realistically, parents knew they had to depend on their offspring for support in their old age as well as for the survival of their family line. It is no wonder that, as noted in the Introduction, the laughter induced by senryu dealing with children is by and large devoid of cynicism and malice.

Children started school when they were six or seven years old. Whereas samurai's sons were tutored privately or went to academies operated by the shogunate or the daimyo they served, children of the plebeian class attended what was called a *terakoya*, a small private school located at a temple or at a teacher's house in their neighborhood. According to a document dated 1722, there were some eight hundred terakoya scattered all over the city of Edo at that time. Interestingly, in the downtown areas almost as many girls as boys went to those schools, presumably so that they could obtain skills needed for helping in family business when they grew up. Lessons given at most terakoya were in reading, calligraphy, arithmetic and, for girls, sewing. More advanced students learned classical Chinese and read major Confucian classics such as *The Analects* and *Mencius*.

There was no special program leading to an academic degree or diploma. How long children would attend terakoya was determined largely by their ability as well as by their family circumstances, but a period of three to four years was the norm.

Children were thought to have come of age when they reached puberty, usually around the age of fourteen. Boys had their forelocks shaved off at a formal ceremony. Girls' families celebrated the occasion by cooking rice mixed with red beans, a custom that still survives in many parts of Japan. Those who were so honored were understandably jubilant, knowing that they could begin enjoying the privileges of an adult. Few realized that the most carefree period of their life was now behind them.

she lets the baby
catch drippings from the eaves
and makes him stop crying

to a baby
crawling into his lap, the priest
shows his prayer beads

amadare wo te ni ukesasete nakiyamase (Y 3)

oshōsama hiza e kuru ko ni juzu wo dashi (Y 4)

home from a journey—
raising his baby on high
he greets his neighbors

the nanny
all dressed up
chasing the naked

tabi modori ko wo sashiagete tonari made (Y 1)

kikazatte uba wa hadaka wo oimawashi (Y 2)

the father calls out
holding up the chessboard
"Nanny, come quick!"

the pediatrician
first takes the pulse
of the stuffed tiger

shōgiban sashiagete ite kore uba yo (Y 5)

shōnika wa tora no myaku nado totte mise (YS 10)

two nannies
confronting each other
over one persimmon[1]

now that he has a child
he knows all the local dogs
by name

[1] An affluent family hired two or more wet nurses, each looking after a different child. Naturally each nurse developed a sense of loyalty to the child she was in charge of. Among several different interpretations this senryu allows, the most popular one asks the reader to visualize a persimmon tree from which one fruit is missing.

uba dōshi taiketsu ni naru kaki hitotsu (Y 4)

ko wo motte kinjo no inu no na wo oboe (YS 9)

the child's message
is supplemented by his mother
through the fence

the pharmacist says
"Come back with the right name"
and sends the child home

ko no tsukai kaki kara haha ga ato wo ii (Yanaibako 2)

kigusuriya kiite kina yo to ko wo kaeshi (Y 6)

"My daddy?
He's dead right now"
says the actor's son[1]

reunited
with his lost child, he says thanks
in a hoarse voice

[1] The little son seems to be playing outside a theater. His words suggest his father is a minor actor always cast in the role of a villain who gets killed by the play's hero, a skilled swordsman.

tossan wa ima shinderu to inari no ko (Y 107)

mayoigo no oya wa shagarete rei wo ii (Y 2)

given some sparklers
they chant, "Go quick, day!"
"Go quick, day!"[1]

the first Horse Day:
parents begin to breathe
a little more easily[2]

[1] This appears to be a parody of a well-known hokku by Buson:

by day, "Go quick, day!"   *hi wa hi kureyo*
by night, "Let it dawn, night!"   *yo wa yo akeyo to*
chant the frogs   *naku kawazu*

[2] Schools customarily started after the first Horse Day (*hatsuuma*) of the lunar second
month.

hanabi wo morai hi ga kurero hi ga kurero (Y 17)

hatsuuma no hi kara fūfu wa chitto iki (SHM: Hōreki 13)

on the alley, school's out—
children everywhere, like hornets
pouring from the nest

if it's not
his medicine, it's a fight—
headache for a mother[1]

[1] A mother who has a healthy son is lucky, as she does not have to worry about medicine.
But she has to worry about the son getting into a fight.

tenaraiko hachi no gotoku ni roji kara de (YS 10)

kusuri no ku senai oya ni wa kenka no ku (Y 1)

first a glare
at her son, then she begins
an apology

his head drooped so low
the reprimand passes
far above it

ko wo hitotsu niramete oite mōshiwake (Y 21)

teitō no ue wo iken wa tōri koshi (Y 138)

someone at the door:
the scolding session
stops—for a while

each time the son
gets a scolding, more people
learn his age

monomō ga atte hitomazu shikari yame (Y 7)

shikarareru tabi ni musuko no toshi ga shire (Y 25)

a bad turn of luck—
the hanger-on is not fond
of children

admired by the mother
whose child is tubercular:
the neighborhood brats

isōrō inga to kodomo kirai nari (Y 24)

rōgai no haha wa kinjo no dora wo home (Y 21)

"Thus spake the Master"—
each time with these words
he gives a cough[1]

each time footsteps
approach, he puts it under
The Analects

DIMPLED LITTLE LUNATICS   159

[1] The child is diligently reciting *The Analects*. Such a studious child is prone to contract tuberculosis.

shi no notamawaku to itte wa seki wo seki (K 1)

ashioto ga suru to rongo no shita e ire (K 2)

how promising!
his son is left cold
by the year's first snow[1]

parent and child
count the year's remaining days
for different reasons[2]

[1] A child who shows interest in the beauties of nature is not likely to become a successful businessman when he grows up.
[2] While the child is happily looking forward to the New Year festivities, the parents struggle to pay off their debts before the end of the year.

hatsuyuki wo homenu musuko ga mono ni nari (YS 1)

kazoebi wa oya no to ko no wa ōchigai (Y 7)

among the things
he teaches his beloved son:
the art of suicide[1]

parents at home
before opening the letter
muse over its bulk[2]

[1] Beyond doubt the father is a man of the samurai class, who has to commit ritual suicide if the occasion requires.
[2] Letters from children always please the parents, but a long letter portends bad news—or else it is a request for money.

hara wo kiru koto wo oshiete kaaigari (YS 9)

kuni no oya fūtai wo mite fū wo kiri (YS 9)

"Is this the child
who used to be a little child
of your child?"

for his poor handwriting
cicadas and dragonflies
take the blame[1]

[1] Hunting insects like cicadas and dragonflies was a favorite pastime for children. The man in this senryu had been so absorbed in it as a child that he neglected his calligraphy lessons.

ano oko no oko ga mō haya kono oko ka (Y 64)

akuhitsu no kōkai semi ya tonbo nari (Y 31)

when she starts to feel
coy, she enters a woman's life
so full of pain[1]

on account
of a parent, no child
has gone insane[2]

[1] As noted in the Introduction, a woman in feudal Japan was forced to play a subservient
role with perseverance throughout her adult life.
[2] Several famous noh plays feature a madwoman looking for her missing child. Yet there is
no major work of literature that describes a child who has gone insane because of his or
her parent. This senryu seems to be a comment on the relative strengths of motherly love and
filial piety, or of a human instinct and a moral principle.

hazukashisa shitte onna no ku no hajime (Y 1)

oya yue ni mayōte wa denu monogurui (Y 1)

6. The Battle of the Generations

In eighteenth-century Japan a married couple normally lived in the same house as the husband's parents. The result was a large household where two or three generations of people spent time together for a number of years. The situation inevitably created tension between the generations, all the more so because a Japanese house architecturally allowed its residents little privacy. Not surprisingly, tension was greatest between father and son, and between mother and daughter-in-law.

The stock image of the father in premodern senryu is one of a hard-working man who has maintained his business in good order for many years. Having spent his entire life in the city, he has urbane hobbies like haikai, the kabuki theater, and the game of Go, and is not averse to seeking pleasure in the amusement quarters, but he is usually mature enough to control his appetites. By contrast, the son is frequently depicted as a prodigal who steals money from his father's business and spends it on his favorite courtesan. Although his father reprimands him sternly, the young man has tasted the pleasures of the demimonde and would not change his lifestyle. Sometimes the angry father has to have a lockup room built in his house and confine the son there. When all his efforts to reform the son fail, the father has no choice but to disown him. Legal disinheritance, however, is rare; usually the son is sent to a relative in the countryside and is allowed to come home upon his repentance. All during this conflict between the father and the son, the mother shows sympathy toward the son and tries to protect him, often to the displeasure of her husband.

The mother, who is all tenderness to her prodigal son, acts like a she-devil toward her virtuous daughter-in-law. Perhaps she hates her son's wife out of possessiveness. Or she is jealous of her youth. Or she wants to take vengeance for past sufferings at the hands of her own in-laws. The son is powerless to protect his poor wife, since feudal morality dictates the absolute submission of children. He can do little even when his parents decide to terminate his marriage. To avoid that kind of crisis, the wife has to silently endure all the torments inflicted by her mother-in-law. Well aware of the situation, writers of senryu are in general sympathetic toward the wife and portray the mother-in-law in a variety of unflattering postures.

the son stays by the fire
while the father goes out
until he slips and falls[1]

curfew at ten—
the first to break it
is the master's son

[1] The senryu is a parody of Bashō's hokku:

now then, let's go out	*iza saraba*
to enjoy the snow—until	*yukimi ni korobu*
I slip and fall	*tokoro made*

Whereas the father is a man of poetic taste who enjoys snowscapes, the son would rather stay warm indoors.

ko wa kotatsu oyaji wa korobu tokoro made (YS 4)

yotsu kiri wo yaburi hajime wa musuko nari (SHM: Meiwa 4)

one wants to save
and the other to spend—
incessant warfare

the saver,
the spender, and between them
the mother

tametagaru tsukaitagaru de fudan mome (Y 10)

kanryaku to taiki no naka ni haha wa tachi (Y 9)

the mother
so like a merciful goddess
and so easy to cheat on

the weapon he uses
for threatening his mother:
a distant land

hahaoya wa mottainai ga damashi yoi (Y 1)

ofukuro wo odosu dōgu wa tōi kuni (Y 1)

"Yes, yes—but still
it's better than gambling"
says the doting mother

little by little
the mother is helping her son
to become a bum

sarinagara utsu ni wa mashi to amai haha (Y 3)

chitto zutsu haha tetsudatte dora ni suru (Y 19)

"And you're as much
to blame"—his mother
gets scolded too

the wife—
so much harder to handle
than the mother

konata made guru da to haha wa shikarareru (Y 10)

nyōbō wa ofukuro yori mo jama na mono (Y 6)

the first time his son
has come home in the morning
he leaves the room[1]

after a big blast
at his eldest son, he goes out
to look for him

[1] The father leaves the room with no reprimand to his son because, while he disapproves
of him spending a night in the pleasure quarters, he also thinks it's part of growing up. It
would be different if the son were to repeat the act too many times.

hajimete wa oyaji ga hazusu asagaeri (SHM: Meiwa 6)

jinroku wo shikari sugoshite tazune ni de (Y 19)

"In that case, it isn't
a game of Go he's playing"
his father knows[1]

his book for noh lessons:
a prop for staging the lie
he tells his father

[1] Playing Go is a good excuse to use for going out, because it takes many hours to complete a game.

sureba go ja nai to oyaji mo mō satori (Y 10)

utaibon oyaji wo bakasu dōgu nari (SHM: An'ei 4)

home in the morning—
his mother shakes her head
as he walks past the gate

home in the morning—
the son first clears away
anything he may be hit with

asagaeri haha no kaburi de yoko e kire (Y 5)

asagaeri tatakaresōna mono wo noke (SHM: Meiwa 6)

the morning glories too
begin to screw up their faces—
such a long scolding!

home in the morning—
although the sky is high
his body hugs the ground

asagao mo tsura wo shikameru naga kogoto (Y 17)

asagaeri ten takakeredo se kugumari (YS 4)

home in the morning—
to show whose side she's on
the maid looks sullen

with a snow shovel
the father lunges; the son
riposts with an umbrella

asagaeri gejo ohamuki ni buninsō (Y 17)

yukikaki de butsu to musuko wa kasa de uke (Y 7)

"Let's eat breakfast"—
the mother tries to restore
peace in the home

while the mother
is away, they hurry to build
a lockup room

asameshi wo mā agareyo to haha nadame (SHM: Meiwa 6)

ofukuro no rusu ni shiageru zashikirō (Y 23)

locked up at home
his dreams roam
the pleasure quarters[1]

locked up at home
the son asks for the beads
to scare his parents[2]

[1] This is a parody of Bashō's deathbed poem:

ailing on a journey	*tabi ni yande*
my dreams roam	*yume wa kareno wo*
a withered moor	*kake meguru*

[2] A man about to commit suicide usually counted his beads and prayed for the peaceful rest of his soul after death.

zashikirō yume ni kuruwa wo kake meguri (Y 53)

zashikirō juzu wo nedatte kowagarase (Y 23)

while he blames
the friend of his son, he doesn't
blame his son

"Don't go out
with that fellow," both fathers
tell their sons

sono tsure wo nikumi sono musuko wo nikumazu (SHM: An'ei 7)

are to deruna to ryōhō no oya ga ii (Y 19)

the suicide note:
he knew he had been
an unfilial son[1]

HOUSE FOR SALE
written in a splendid
calligraphic hand[2]

[1] "I am sorry I have been such an unfilial son" was a stock sentence used in a suicide note.
[2] The owner of the house is a man with artistic talents, which means he has no talent for making money.

kakioki wo mireba fukō mo shitte iru (Y 13)

appare na te de urisue to kaite hari (YS 10)

her only pleasures:
tormenting the daughter-in-law
and visiting the temple

while her mouth recites
prayers, her eyes shoot daggers
at her daughter-in-law

tanoshimi wa yome wo ibiru to tera mairi (Y 17)

kuchi ni shōmyō manako ni wa yome wo neme (Y 21)

no harsh words—
she just praises a neighbor's
daughter-in-law

the mother-in-law
slips back into her usual face
when the guest leaves

shikarazu ni tonari no yome wo homete oki (YS 9)

shūtobaba kyaku ga kaeru to moto no tsura (SHM: Meiwa 4)

the mother-in-law
bathes in the sun, her face
turned toward the house

a marvelous wife
beloved by her mother-in-law
does not live long

shūtome no hinatabokko wa uchi wo muki (Y 2)

shūtome no ki ni iru yome wa yo ga hayashi (Y 4)

thanks to her cruelties
her son is a bachelor
once again

the mother-in-law
reveals her warped head
on becoming a nun[1]

[1] The mother-in-law has died and had her head shaven, as was the custom in some sects of Buddhism.

ibitte wa musuko wo hitorimono ni suru (Y 21)

shūtome no tsumuji wa ama ni natte shire (Y 1)

7. Playboys of the Floating World

Edo was a big city that provided a great variety of entertainments and amusements. The amusement facilities, however, were by and large for the benefit of the male residents, who numbered almost twice as many as the women. While women could enjoy few diversions beyond theatergoing, blossom viewing, and other seasonal festivities, men were free to go and carouse in the amusement districts, such as those located in Ryōgoku, Ueno, and Asakusa. They could also spend a night with a courtesan in one of the pleasure quarters, most notably Yoshiwara, if they were willing to risk the ire of their fathers and wives. Some of them, who called themselves *ukiyo otoko* (men of the floating world), actually took pride in their knowledge of and experience in the various pleasures available in the city. To their way of thinking, men might as well enjoy life in any way they could, since the world they lived in was rapidly floating away.

Theatrical entertainments in eighteenth-century Edo included the noh, the kabuki, and the puppet drama as well as less refined types of popular theater. Whereas the noh was staged almost exclusively for the samurai class, all the other types of theater were available to townspeople capable of paying the admission. It is believed that Edoites spent a total of one thousand ryō each day for theatrical entertainments, including the cost of food and drink consumed in and around the theaters. The kabuki, which was performed on a large indoor stage, was especially popular in Edo and its main actors determined the fashions of the day. But there were only three kabuki theaters in the city during much of the eighteenth century, and it was too expensive for ordinary townsfolk to go there frequently. More often they went to smaller and cheaper theaters located in the amusement districts or in some temporary quarters. At those places spectators would eat a meal, drink sake, and even watch a brawl in the gallery—all while a performance was in progress on stage.

Edo had several bawdy-house districts within its borders, but Yoshiwara was the largest and also the only place of its kind that was licensed by the government. Located in the northern part of the city, it was encircled by a moat that was connected to canals and rivers so that customers could reach it by boat if they wanted to. Young women who worked in the quarter, known as *geisha* or courtesans, were of all ranks and prices depending on their qualifications. Geisha literally means an "accomplished person," and indeed the highest-ranking courtesans were not only attractive in appearance but also accomplished in music, dance, flower arrangement, calligraphy, and other arts. The great majority of townsmen, however, could only afford courtesans who ranked at or near the bottom of the scale and who were little different from ordinary prostitutes. Geisha of this class were mostly daughters of impoverished peasants and townsmen who had to sacrifice themselves for their families; they usually served a term of ten years in exchange for a lump-sum payment made to their families in advance. Supposedly their customers were exclusively men of the plebeian class, for samurai were expected to conduct themselves according to the highest standard of morality. But in actuality many samurai as well as Buddhist priests disguised themselves and frequented the brothel districts, as alluded to in some of the senryu that appeared in the earlier sections of this book.

a teahouse where
the tea costs as much as sake—
she's that good-looking

at the footsteps
the topic of conversation
changes

sake no nedan ni cha no ureru utsukushisa (K 4)

ashioto ga suru to hanashi no dai wo kae (YS 2)

the instant
he sobers up, he begins
concocting a story

starting to kill himself
the actor stops to watch a fight
in the audience

yoi ga sameru to uso wo tsuku kufû nari (SHM: An'ei 5)

hara wo kiri kakete kenka wo kenbutsu shi (Y 52)

after smartening up
the whole village, it leaves—
a traveling troupe

that monk on the noh stage—
he looks as if he could use
an ashtray[1]

PLAYBOYS OF THE FLOATING WORLD

[1] In many noh plays a traveling monk introduces the main actor and then sits in a corner of
the stage for the rest of the play.

hitomura wo sui ni shite tatsu tabishibai (Y 2)

wakisō wa tabakobon de mo hoshiku mie (Y 3)

guessing the action
from far back in the gallery
they weep with the rest[1]

the streetwalker
with his torn sleeve in her hand:
"Oh sir, I'm sorry!"

[1] A scene in the kabuki theater. Cheap seats are so far back that those who sit there cannot see the stage very well.

suiryō de mukōsajiki no morainaki (Y 5)

tomeonna katasode motte wabite iru (Y 3)

Yoshiwara—
that's where a man goes to dump
all his better judgment

when the night falls
the day starts to break
on the brothels

Yoshiwara e otoko no chie wo sute ni yuki (YS 7)

yo no naka wa kurete kuruwa wa hiru ni nari (YS 6)

a filial daughter
and an unfilial son
sleeping side by side

a new client:
the courtesan tries to guess
his age and business

kō fukō futatsu naraberu nurimakura (SHM: Meiwa 6)

shokai no yo mazu shōbai to toshi wo ate (Y 32)

even her smile
is carefully made up—
the courtesan

with wriggling worms
for bait, the courtesan
fishes for men[1]

[1] Earthworms were often used as a metaphor for women's handwriting, which usually contained many hiragana, the more cursive of the two Japanese syllabaries. Courtesans sometimes wrote letters to their customers to ask them for more frequent visits.

waraigao made keisei wa koshiraeru (Y 13)

notakutta mimizu wo esa ni kyaku wo tsuri (Y 38)

the romantic letter
smells of her greed—
how unromantic!

each time her letter
arrives, the son must show
his sleight of hand

tamazusa ni yoku ga majitte gebiru nari (SHM: An'ei 4)

fumi no kuru tanbi ni musuko chie wo dashi (H 23)

it hurts him too
when her request comes enclosed
with a little finger[1]

the courtesan's tears
pound on his storehouse roof
till it begins to leak

[1] To show loyalty to a customer, a courtesan sometimes cut off the tip of her little finger.

itai koto koyubi ni kaketa mushin nari (Y 39)

keisei no namida de kura no yane ga mori (YS 6)

his wife worries
when the cherry blossoms bloom
when the moon shows off[1]

though the blossoms
said nothing, his wife somehow
has learned of it

[1] She worries at those times because her husband has a ready-made excuse to go out and visit the pleasure quarters.

nyōbō no ku wa hana ga saki tsuki ga sashi (Y 10)

hana mono wo iwanedo nyōbo kedoru nari (Y 8)

"You saw the blossoms
then you saw . . . ," his angry wife
screams at him

a clever wife:
she makes him take their child
on his blossom viewing

hana wo mite soshite to nyōbo itakedaka (Y 160)

nyōbō no chie wa hanami ni ko wo tsukeru (Y 10)

maple viewing:
nowadays, it's a courtesan
who casts the spell[1]

"Just dead leaves"
he says, passing right by
Shōtō Temple

[1] In the noh play *Momijigari* (Maple Viewing), a general who goes to the mountains for maple viewing encounters a charming lady, who turns out to be a she-devil in disguise. Two popular places for maple viewing in Edo were Shōtō Temple and Kaian Temple, both of which happened to be in close proximity to pleasure quarters.

momijigari ima wa yūjo ga taburakashi (Y 24)

Shōtōji nani kareppa to sugu tōri (Y 6)

maple viewing:
nowadays, the she-devil waits
at home

maple viewing:
his mother tells him not to do
what he did last year

momijigari ima wa hannya ga uchi de machi (Y 57)

momijimi ni haha wa kyonen no iken wo shi (Y 3)

glasses for the eyes
and dentures for the teeth
but what for the third?[1]

"My old man
still wants to go north
instead of west"[2]

[1] It was popularly believed that an aging man's physical decline began with the eyes, the teeth, and the sexual drive, in that order.
[2] Yoshiwara was located in the northern part of the city. The Buddhist paradise was believed to lie in the west.

me wa megane ha wa ireba ni te ma ni aedo (Y 38)

oyaji mada nishi yori kita e yuku ki nari (Y 5)

he loves his grandson
but goes out to buy someone
he loves more

"I'm completely
back to health," says a man
whose nose has dropped off[1]

[1] It seems that the man had syphilis.

mago yori wa kāii sō de kai ni yuki (H 2)

suppari to naorimashita to hana ga ochi (Y 16)

he awakes
only after his parents
have gone to sleep

as he smiles
at the nun without a finger
she only smiles[1]

[1] It seems that the nun was formerly a courtesan. She must have gone through some very painful experiences; otherwise she would not have become a nun. But through the help of religion she has been able to put all that past life behind her, and now she does not even have an urge to tell her story to others.

oyatachi ga nemutta ato de me ga sameru (Y 61)

yubi no nai ama wo waraeba warau nomi (Y 1)

8. Let Us Laugh with the Seasons

Edo townsmen, like other Japanese, were sensitive to the passage of time and the accompanying changes in nature. Buddhism, which stressed the transitoriness of all things, and Shintoism, which originated in nature worship, were part of the reason. More importantly, Edo's geographical location guaranteed a cycle of the four seasons that brought clearly visible changes to the natural environment. Furthermore, throughout the year there were many seasonal festivities in which all city residents participated. People were constantly reminded of the season, of the fact that the basic rhythm of their life was based on the seasonal cycle that regulated all things on earth. It is no wonder that haikai, a popular form of poetry in the eighteenth century, started with a verse that included a word implying the season of the year. Senryu, which branched off from haikai, also made frequent use of seasonal topics, even though it was not required to use a kigo.

The most festive day of the year was New Year's Day, which would have fallen in late January or early February in the Gregorian calendar. It was not only the beginning of the year but a birthday for every Japanese, who grew one year older on that day according to the traditional way of counting. The day was also a Shinto holiday, on which people visited a local shrine early in the morning and prayed for good fortune during the coming year. Later in the day they visited their personal friends and professional colleagues to exchange greetings. For merchants, the day marked the beginning of a new fiscal year, which meant that all outstanding debts had to be paid off by New Year's Eve. Writers of senryu were especially amused by the various ingenious ways in which some townsmen tried to tide themselves over this critical time.

After the New Year, Edo residents in the eighteenth century observed a great number of seasonal festivities one after another: the Girls' Festival in the third month, the Boys' Festival in the fifth month, the Star Festival in the seventh month, the Ebisu Festival in the tenth month, to mention only a few. Some of those events are still celebrated in Tokyo today. Yet many others were discontinued years ago, since they were closely connected with the religious and folk beliefs of the past. The communal spirit has diminished in modern times, too. Consequently, the senryu that draw on annual observances have in many cases become difficult for today's readers to understand, even with explanatory notes.

More understandable are the senryu that deal with the beauty of nature — cherry blossoms, young leaves, summer showers, the harvest moon, snowscapes. Of course those were staple subjects in haikai, yet writers of senryu observed them with a distinctly different focus. Instead of admiring the beauty of cherry blossoms, for instance, they poked fun at picnickers who seemed to be enjoying the sake more than the flowers. They were interested less in colorful autumn leaves than in young maple viewers who took the opportunity to visit the nearby pleasure quarters. A sudden shower, another common topic in haikai, was also a favored subject for senryu writers because it gave them a chance for humorous observation.

Edo townsmen took notice of the passage of time not only through the eye but also through the palate. Traditional Japanese culinary art required that a sense of the season be created at all times. Fresh food in season was easily available in Edo, which could draw on wide farming areas to the north and the Pacific Ocean to the south. Of the many kinds of food that appear in senryu, two fish are especially conspicuous because of their frequent mention: bonito and *fugu* (blowfish). Bonito was caught and sold only in summer, so that it brought a keen sense of the season with it. Because it tasted best in early summer, it was in great demand and commanded an exorbitant price at that time. Fugu, on the other hand, was eaten only during the cold months. The meat was most delicious, but had to be cooked with the utmost care because some of the fish's internal organs contained deadly poison. Today the poisonous parts as well as the nature of the poison have been scientifically identified, and licensed experts alone are permitted to cook the fish. But in premodern times anyone who had the money could buy and cook it for dinner, and many daring souls did so—some losing their lives as a result.

New Year's Day:
without ceremony, he
resurrects himself[1]

perhaps he owes
some money—his New Year's greeting
is too cordial

[1] Not being able to pay off his debts, the man apparently has had his wife tell his creditors
that he is dead.

ganjitsu ni ike shāshā to yomigaeri (YS 1)

kari ga aru sō de gyokei ni nen ga iri (Y 22)

the tune is familiar:
"Happy New Year!"—as only
drunkards say it[1]

on plum blossoms,
bush warblers; under cherry
blossoms, drunkards[2]

[1] People served food and drink for those who came to offer New Year's greetings.
[2] A bush warbler perched on a blossoming plum tree is a traditional motif in Japanese art.

namayoi wa gyokei ni fushi wo tsukete ii (Y 3)

ume ni uguisu sakura ni namaei nari (Y 18)

asleep on the ground
holding a spray of blossoms
an elegant drunkard

"Won't bring you again!" —
the nondrinkers tie him up
to a cherry tree

hana no eda motte fūga na taoremono (Y 6)

nido to wa tsurenu to sakura e geko kukushi (Y 20)

it costs nothing
for the eye and ear, but a lot
for the mouth[1]

early summer:
mumbling "Life is short"
he buys a bonito

[1] This senryu alludes to a famous hokku by Yamaguchi Sodō (1642–1716) that cites the three great pleasures offered by nature in early summer:

green leaves for the eye	*me ni aoba*
cuckoos in the forest	*yama hototogisu*
and the first bonito	*hatsugatsuo*

me mo hana mo tada da ga kuchi wa takaku tsuki (SHM: Tenmei 2)

hatsugatsuo ningen wazuka nazo to kau (SHM: Meiwa 5)

in early summer
they eat gold coins
flavored with miso[1]

he buys a bonito
together with six months' worth
of his wife's griping

[1] The most common way to eat an early summer bonito was to slice the meat and eat it raw. Ordinarily *miso* (bean paste) mixed with vinegar was used as the condiment.

shigatsu jōjun ni koban wo miso de kui (Y 25)

hatsugatsuo nyōbo ni kohantoshi iware (Y 15)

"A bonito
is better than a courtesan"
says his resigned wife

at street corners
they're selling lukewarm water—
what a hot day![1]

LET US LAUGH WITH THE SEASONS

---

[1] "Cold water" is what the signs say, but the water is not cold.

jorō yori mada mo katsuo to nyōbo ii (Y 29)

nurumayu wo tsuji tsuji de uru atsui koto (Y 13)

when the water-seller
is an old man, the water
does not look cold

midsummer visitors
make him flee, with a pillow
and a fan[1]

[1] While *shochū mimai* (midsummer greetings) are exchanged with postcards today, the custom in premodern Japan required people to pay a courtesy visit in person during the hot season. With no telephone or e-mail, such a visit was made unannounced.

mizuuri mo jijii wa nurui yō ni mie (K 4)

shoki mimai makura to uchiwa motte nige (Y 12)

midsummer airing:
someone is standing watch
by taking a nap[1]

"I'm here, Mom"
she answers, taking some air
outside the garden gate[2]

[1] On a fine summer day after the rainy season, people brought out bedding, clothes, books, and all kinds of other things to the front yard and aired them all day long.
[2] Some young girls went out to join their boyfriends on summer evenings after telling their mothers they were going out to cool themselves in the night air.

yōjin ni hirune shite iru doyōboshi (Y 4)

koko ni oriyasu to musume no kado suzumi (Y 10)

sheltering from rain
he's memorized all the words
on the plaque[1]

till the rain lets up
he haggles over the price
of an umbrella

[1] It seems that the man has taken shelter under the roofed gate of an old temple or some such structure of historical significance.

amayadori gaku no monji wo yoku oboe (Y 1)

ame no yamu uchi karakasa wo negitte i (YS 9)

he asks the price
of things he doesn't want
till the rain stops

sheltering from rain—
now and then he steps out to see
how wet he gets

iri mo senu mono no ne wo kiku amayadori (Y 3)

amayadori chotcho to dete wa nurete miru (Y 13)

he takes shelter
then, after it's begun to pour,
decides to leave

off with the new pawn!
on with the old! here comes
a red dragonfly[1]

[1] In the premodern Japanese poetic tradition, a red dragonfly signified the arrival of autumn. For some townsfolk, it also indicated the time to bring summer clothes to the pawnshop in exchange for the winter clothes kept there during the summer.

honburi ni natte dete yuku amayadori (Y 1)

irekae no saisoku ni kuru akatonbo (YS 9)

so many samples
of crabbed handwriting
start to flow on the eighth[1]

only a grass blade
when I trap it; when I let go
it's a grasshopper

[1] On the night of the Star Festival, held on the seventh day of the lunar seventh month,
people would write down their wishes on strips of paper and tie the strips to a bamboo
erected in front of their house. The next day the whole display was thrown into a river.

akuhitsu no yatara nagareru yōka sugi (Y 23)

osaereba susuki hanaseba kirigirisu (YS 1)

for the harvest moon
the landlord's gift amounts to
fifteen bullets[1]

going to the outhouse
and finding it occupied
he admires the moon

[1] A custom in Edo prescribed that a landlord give out sweet dumplings to his tenants on the night of the harvest moon. Apparently the landlord in this senryu is a stingy man, for his dumplings are not much larger than bullets.

ōya kara teppōdama ga jūgo kuru (Y 12)

setchin e saki wo kosarete tsuki wo home (YS 1)

now then, let's go out
to enjoy the moon—until we stumble
upon a tavern[1]

tinted leaves—
now the temple is anything
but a temple[2]

[1] This is another parody of Bashō's hokku:

now then, let's go out	*iza saraba*
to enjoy the snow—until	*yukimi ni korobu*
I slip and fall	*tokoro made*

[2] As in blossom viewing, people who went out to view the fall colors on the grounds of a temple would enjoy themselves by eating and drinking under the trees.

iza saraba tsukimi ni nomeru tokoro made (Y 54)

kigi somete tera wo tera ni wa shite okazu (Y 30)

the Ebisu Festival—
for the next four or five days
they have to suck the bones[1]

"How manly!" they praised him
but the scar from that incident
makes him predict snow[2]

[1] On the day of the Ebisu Festival, which was usually the twentieth of the lunar tenth month, merchants invited their important customers to their homes and treated them to banquets that featured sea breams. "They" in this senryu refers to the store clerks and other employees.
[2] Often a scar aches in cold and damp weather, especially before a snowfall. The man in this senryu belatedly found out that such an ache was the price he had to pay for his badge of courage.

ebisukō shigonichi hone wo shaburaseru (Y 10)

otoko ja to iwareta kizu ga yuki wo shiri (Y 1)

with a black dog
for a lantern, he walks
along the snowy path

footprints in the snow:
all that remains of those
bloody fools[1]

[1] This is a parody of Bashō's famous hokku:

summer grasses—	natsugusa ya
all that remains of those	tsuwamonodomo ga
warriors' dreams	yume no ato

The "bloody fools" in the senryu are people of poetic taste who went out snow viewing early in the morning.

kuroinu wo chōchin ni suru yuki no michi (Y 1)

kono yuki ni bakamonodomo no ashi no ato (Y 79)

"Anyone willing
to die with me?" asks the man
buying a fugu[1]

what a coward!
he eats nothing but the radish
in the fugu soup

[1] Some fugu are too big for one person to eat. "Anyone willing to die with me?" mimicks the
words of a samurai leader asking for volunteers on a dangerous mission.

mō hoka ni shinite nashi ka to fugu wo kai (Y 8)

okubyō na koto daikon wo kutte iru (Y 15)

fugu soup:
there are fools who eat it
there are fools who don't

for the rest of his life
he's resented by the widow—
the fugu seller

fugujiru wo kuwanu tawake ni kū tawake (YS 1)

fugu uri wa isshō goke ni uramirare (Y 65)

when they've finished
praising the winter moon
they slam the door on it

the last month of the year:
before scolding someone
he counts the days[1]

[1] Townspeople were busy and irritable during the last month of the year, as they had to prepare for the year to come. While venting their irritation, they often said something like "Remember, there're only eight more days until New Year's Day!"

fuyu no tsuki hometarikeri de patari tate (Y 6)

jūnigatsu hito wo shikaru ni hi wo kazoe (Y 4)

year-end shopping:
on his list, a fern, a pine
and a courtesan[1]

with salted salmon
the one attacks; with persimmons
the other counters[2]

[1] The biggest year-end fair in Edo was held in Asakusa, near Yoshiwara. A fern and a pine sapling were used for New Year decorations.
[2] The end of the year was—and still is—a time for exchanging gifts. The bothersome custom is here compared to a battle.

kaimono wa urajiro nematsu jorō nari (Y 13)

shiobiki de utte kakareba kaki de uke (YS 1)

before going stale
a sea bream does its duty
at four or five houses[1]

rice cake has been made—
all that remains to be made
is lies for the creditors[2]

[1] Sometimes a family that received a gift such as a sea bream from another family passed it on to a third family, pretending it was a newly bought gift.
[2] Rice cake is for the New Year's celebration.

kusatte mo tai wa shigoken tsutomete ki (SHM: Meiwa 8)

mochi wa tsuku kore kara uso wo tsuku bakari (Y 1)

his wife knows
how to scare a collector:
"He's down with typhoid"

the last day of the year—
his lies stir the feelings
of gods and spirits[1]

[1] In extolling the affective power of poetry, the famous preface to *Kokin waka shū* (The Collection of Ancient and Modern Poems) says: "It is poetry that, without effort, stirs the feelings of invisible gods and spirits."

kaketori e naigi shōkan da to odoshi (YS 1)

ōmisoka uso de kijin wo kanzeshime (YS 1)

9. Heroes
Without Halos

There are many senryu that poke fun at illustrious figures of the past. Obviously those who wrote them were well-read in history and literature, and so were the contemporary readers for whom they were intended. Books had become more easily available to ordinary people since the early seventeenth century, as rapid progress was made in printing techniques. It is estimated that during the eighteenth century book dealers in Edo sold some six thousand titles. People who could not afford to buy books borrowed them from commercial book lenders for a small rental fee. The fact that Edo had as many as seven hundred lending libraries within city limits in the late eighteenth century suggests how large the reading population was at that time. The most popular books were illustrated works of fiction, but books in other genres, such as history and classical literature, boasted a good number of readers too.

History as learned by Edo townsmen, however, was not much more than a loose sequence of historical episodes featuring interesting people and events. Schoolchildren were first exposed to history through letters and documents dealing with famous men and women. Little attention was paid to factual accuracy, since the main purpose of using those materials in the classroom was to have the children learn moral lessons along with reading and writing. The first publication that resembles a history textbook came out in 1775, but even that was only a collection of didactic anecdotes loosely put together in chronological order. When those children grew up, they expanded their knowledge of history by reading historical literature as well as by watching kabuki and puppet plays, many of which drew on history. Although few townsmen had a chance to see the noh drama performed on the stage, melodious recitation of noh texts was a common pastime among them, and many leading characters of the noh were historical figures.

Edo townspeople gained a knowledge of classical literature in similar ways. Some may have read classics like *Kojiki* and *Genji monogatari* (The Tale of Genji) in the original, because those texts had become available in printed editions since the early seventeenth century. Yet most of the people acquired a general knowledge of the classics through the noh, the kabuki, the puppet theater, and popular fiction. War stories, such as *Heike monogatari* (The Tale of the Heike) and *Taiheiki* (The Record of Great Peace), were retold in an entertaining manner by professional storytellers. *Hyakunin isshu* (One Hundred Poems by One Hundred Poets), a waka anthology compiled by Fujiwara Teika (1161–1241), had been transformed into a card game and had won great popularity among commoners by the mid-eighteenth century. Because many senryu writers apparently wrote haikai as well, they were familiar with representative haikai verses of past masters such as Matsuo Bashō and Takarai Kikaku (1661–1707). All in all, they had an extensive knowledge of literature both classical and modern, even though few were scholars who had studied it systematically.

even in the age
of the gods, the day didn't break
without a woman[1]

an ancient god too
when he tricked someone
made use of drink[2]

[1] In a myth recorded in *Kojiki*, the sun goddess Amaterasu hid herself in a cave when her brother Susanoo became too violent to control. To entice her out of the cave and restore daylight to the world, other gods had a certain female deity dance a comic dance in front of the cave. Hearing loud applause, the curious sun goddess opened the cave door slightly, whereupon a powerful male deity opened the door all the way and had her come out of the cave.

[2] In another myth that appears in *Kojiki*, a big eight-headed serpent victimized local maidens in Izumo Province (Shimane Prefecture), until the god Susanoo got it drunk with sake and killed it.

kamiyo de mo onna de nakerya yo ga akezu (Y 124)

kamiyo ni mo damasu kufū wa sake ga iri (Y 1)

the monster serpent
had a passion for both—
that was his downfall

no sacred sword
if the serpent had not been
a thirsty soul[1]

---

[1] The sacred sword is one of the Three Treasures of the Imperial House. It is said to have been discovered in the tail of the big serpent slain by Susanoo.

dotchira mo suki de daija wa shite yarare (YS 5)

hōken wa orochi geko nara ima ni dezu (YS 4)

after a while
the ambassador to T'ang
longs for rice with tea[1]

In Chuangtzu's case
his dreams roamed
a flowering field[2]

[1] Japan sent ambassadors and other envoys to China from the seventh century through the ninth century. The author of this senryu imagines that as time passed those envoys must have grown tired of rich Chinese dishes and longed for simple Japanese food.
[2] This alludes to Bashō's deathbed hokku:

ailing on a journey	*tabi ni yande*
my dreams roam	*yume wa kareno wo*
a withered moor	*kakemeguru*

In a famous Taoist tale, Chuangtzu became a butterfly in his dream.

kentōshi ato wa chazuke wo kuitagari (Y 22)

Sōshi no wa yume ga hanano wo kakemeguri (Y 74)

"Mom, are we
moving again?" asked
little Mencius[1]

Mencius's mother—
I'd rather not have her
for my mother-in-law

[1] In the Confucian tradition, Mencius's mother was considered a model parent because of
what she did for her child's education. When Mencius was small his home was located
near a graveyard, which prompted him to amuse himself by playing at funerals. His
alarmed mother moved their residence to a place near a market, whereupon her son
began imitating a merchant. She finally settled down near a school.

okkasan mata kosu no ka to Mōshi ii (Y 37)

saredomo Mōbo shūto ni wa iyana hito (Y 145)

the Seven Sages
sitting pretty through
the big one[1]

the Seven Sages
spent most of their time
fighting mosquitoes[2]

[1] The Seven Sages of the Bamboo Grove were Yüan Chi and six other Taoists of the Tsin dynasty who renounced the world and lived as hermits in a bamboo grove. This senryu implies that they must have remained calm even at the time of a big earthquake, not so much because they were enlightened people unafraid of death as because the ground in a bamboo grove, reenforced by strong roots, is known to be one of the safest places to be when an earthquake strikes.
[2] Mosquitoes are fond of dark, windless places like bamboo groves.

shichiken wa heiki de kurasu ōjishin (Y 103)

shichinin wa yabuka wo ou ni kakatte i (YS 4)

at each footnote
Ch'e Yin gave a good shake
to the fireflies[1]

"Don't bother me"—
Ch'e Yin gave a firefly
to a child who came to play

[1] Ch'e Yin of the Chin dynasty, when he was young and poor, caught fireflies and put them in a cage, which he used for light when he read books at night. Fireflies emit a brighter light when they are disturbed.

chū wo yomu toki ni hotaru wa yusuburare (Y 39)

gakumon no jama da to hotaru hitotsu yari (YS 4)

there is no need
to build a stone monument
for Lady Matsura[1]

poor Lady Matsura!
all her tears have turned
to gravel

[1] Lady Matsura was a young woman who lived in northern Kyushu during the sixth century. Legend has it that when her lover left for Korea she grieved so much that she turned into a stone on a hill overlooking the channel between Japan and Korea.

sono mama de sekihi mo iranu Matsuragata (Y 149)

Matsurahime namida wa minna jari ni nari (YS 5)

"And at a brush store
he has an enormous debt"
Tokihira said[1]

when the sky
cleared, Toki was there
Hira was here[2]

[1] Fujiwara Tokihira (871–909) was a statesman who is said to have resorted to slander
when he ousted his political rival, Sugawara Michizane (845–903), in 901. Michizane was
a renowned calligrapher.
[2] Because of Tokihira's slander, Michizane was exiled to Kyushu. According to legend,
Michizane after his death became a thunder god and returned to Kyoto, where he struck
Tokihira with a thunderbolt and tore him to pieces.

fudeya nado kari ga arō to Shihei ii (YS 5)

seiten ni nari soko ni Toki koko ni Hira (Y 54)

what a miracle
that disease never caught up
with Narihira![1]

in Narihira's time
no woman ever fell in love
for money[2]

[1] The amorous adventures of Arihara Narihira (825–880), a poet and court nobleman,
were fictionalized in *Ise monogatari*.
[2] *Ise monogatari* describes Narihira as being handsome, elegantly mannered, and poetically
talented, but not as being rich.

Narihira no kasa wo kakanu mo fushigi nari (Y 4)

Narihira no jibun kane ni wa horete nashi (Yanaibako 4)

praying for rain—
again it was the woman
who used more words[1]

Lady Murasaki
was by some mistaken for
a priest's mistress[2]

[1] One of the two famous Japanese poems that pray for rain is the following waka by Ono Komachi, a ninth-century noblewoman:

should there be a god	*chihayaburu*
looking over this earth	*kami mo mimaseba*
please hurry	*tachi sawagi*
to open the floodgate	*ame no togawa no*
of the River of Heaven	*higuchi ake tamae*

The other poem is a hokku by Takarai Kikaku, cited later in this section. Waka consists of thirty-one syllables; hokku, of seventeen.

[2] According to legend, Lady Murasaki (978?–1016?) wrote part of *Genji monogatari* at Ishiyama Temple near Lake Biwa.

amagoi mo onna wa tanto kuchi wo kiki (Y 6)

daikoku no yō ni Murasaki Shikibu mie (Y 6)

on that day
Kiyomori had to eat
a second supper[1]

the doctor disrobed
before he went in to take
Kiyomori's pulse[2]

[1] Taira Kiyomori (1118–1181) was a politician of enormous power and influence. According to legend, one day he even called back the setting sun by beckoning it with his fan.
[2] Kiyomori died of an illness accompanied by an extremely high fever.

Kiyomori mo sono hi ni yashoku nido kurai (Y 32)

Kiyomori no isha wa hadaka de myaku wo tori (Y 1)

"Cockroach on board!"
the former Empress and her suite
all stood up[1]

that Tsugunobu—
he too thought nine times out of ten
the arrow would miss him[2]

[1] The "former Empress" referred to here is Kenreimon' in (1159–1213), a daughter of Taira Kiyomori who married Emperor Takakura. Chased by the soldiers of the rival Minamoto clan, members of the Taira family had to flee to the Inland Sea.
[2] In one of the battles between the two clans, the young general Minamoto Yoshitsune (1159–1189) was confronted by a renowned archer. Moments before he was shot at, his loyal retainer Satō Tsugunobu (1158–1185) stepped in front of him and got killed. The incident made Tsugunobu a model of self-sacrifice.

funamushi ni mon'in hajime sō ni tachi (YS 5)

Tsugunobu mo tō ga kokonotsu ataranu ki (Y 8)

boy dolls and girl dolls
in one great festival
dead at Dannoura[1]

"Do as you see fit"—
saying those words was Yoritomo's
one great achievement[2]

[1] The last battle between the Minamoto and Taira clans was fought off the coast of
Dannoura, the western end of Honshu, in 1185. Defeated in the battle, most of the Taira
soldiers, courtiers, and court ladies threw themselves into the sea and perished. The Boys'
Festival, held on the fifth day of the lunar fifth month, was celebrated by displaying dolls
of warriors in arms. The Girls' Festival, observed on the third day of the third month, featured dolls representing courtiers and court ladies.
[2] Minamoto Yoritomo (1147–1199) founded the first shogunate in 1192, after the rival Taira
clan perished at Dannoura. However, it was not he but his younger brothers and other relatives who had actually gone to the battlefield and won the battles for their clan.

sangatsu to gogatsu no yō na Dannoura (Y 29)

yoki ni hakarae de Yoritomo yaku wa sumi (Y 14)

frogs and bush warblers
both lose their voices when they live
on Mount Ogura[1]

crying and crying
in Teika's front yard—
a bush warbler

[1] *Hyakunin isshu*, a famous collection of one hundred waka selected by Fujiwara Teika, includes not one poem on frogs or bush warblers, both popular subjects in Japanese poetry. Teika's house was located on Mt. Ogura in Kyoto.

uguisu mo kawazu mo nakanu Ogurayama (Y 56)

Sadaie no kado ni uguisu naite iru (Y 13)

"Show me a dance" —
such a modest demand to make
on a heavenly maiden![1]

when Lord Kusunoki
gave field commands, he held his nose
between his fingers[2]

[1] In the noh play *Hagoromo* (The Feather Robe), a fisherman picks up a robe left
inadvertently by a heavenly maiden, who cannot fly back home without it. To her plea,
he responds that he would return the robe if she were to dance a heavenly dance for him.
[2] Kusunoki Masashige (?–1336) was a general famous for his military strategies. Once
when his castle was attacked, he had his men spray raw sewage over the enemy soldiers
trying to climb up the outer walls of his castle.

tennin no mai to wa katai yusuri yō (Y 1)

Masashige wa hana wo fusaide zai wo furi (YS 5)

Lord Nobunaga:
the best monkey trainer
in all of Japan[1]

to their sleepy eyes
the ronin seemed to number
four hundred and seven[2]

[1] Oda Nobunaga (1534–1582) was a warlord who succeeded in unifying most of Japan in the late sixteenth century. His chief retainer was Toyotomi Hideyoshi (1536–1598), nicknamed the Monkey, who was born a peasant but rose to become ruler of Japan after Nobunaga's death.
[2] In one of the most famous incidents in Japanese history, forty-seven ronin from the Akō fief attacked and killed Kira Yoshinaka (1640–1702) to avenge their late lord. The people in the Kira household had been asleep on the night of the attack.

Nobunaga wa Nippon ichi no sarutsukai (Y 103)

neboketa de shihyaku shichinin hodo ni mie (Y 11)

the priest in charge
saw more widows than even he
ever wanted to see[1]

can they be praising
Kikaku's verse? the rain frogs
have begun to croak[2]

---

[1] Forty-six of the forty-seven ronin died by performing ritual suicide a couple of months after their successful revenge. Hinted at in this senryu is the alleged penchant of Buddhist priests for seducing young widows.

[2] As mentioned before, Takarai Kikaku prayed for rain during a drought by dedicating the following hokku to a shrine in Edo:

let it shower, please,	yūdachi ya
if there is a god watching	ta wo mimeguri no
over the ricefields	kami naraba

According to Kikaku's own account, it rained the following day.

sono toki no oshō wa goke no miaki wo shi (YS 5)

ku wo homeru yō ni kawazu wa naki idashi (Y 19)

by his own lies
he's moved to tears—
that fellow Chikamatsu[1]

the following year
Chiyo planted the flower
far from the well[2]

[1] Chikamatsu Monzaemon wrote a number of moving plays for the puppet stage. He is reported to have said: "One who writes a puppet play attempts to describe facts as they are, yet in doing so one writes things which are not real but which belong to the realm of art."
[2] Chiyo (1703–1775) is famous for her hokku:

my well-bucket
taken by the morning glory
I borrow water

asagao ni
tsurube torarete
moraimizu

waga uso de kanrui nagasu Monzaemon (YS 9)

yokutoshi wa Chiyo idobata wo satte ue (Y 119)

10. The Way of the Townsman

Just as samurai had a code of ethics called Bushidō prescribing how a warrior was to conduct himself in all phases of life, so commoners in the eighteenth century were guided by a set of moral principles known as *chōnindō* or the Way of the Townsman, although those principles were not as clearly defined or as uniformly accepted. Saikaku's *Nippon eitaigura* (Eternal Storehouse of Japan), published in 1688, already suggests the emergence of a moral code distinctly different from Bushidō, since it portrays many merchants who have singlemindedly devoted themselves to the pursuit of wealth. In fact, the book was subtitled *Daifuku shin chōjakyō* (The Bible for Happy New Millionaires), indicating, albeit humorously, that it contained essential teachings of a new school of thought. Such mercantilism, clearly incompatible with Confucian morality, gained further support among commoners during the decades that followed, as the commercial economy grew stronger and made their daily lives more comfortable. In his book *Sundai zatsuwa* (Sundai Miscellanies, 1732) the Confucian scholar Muro Kyūsō (1658–1734) laments that in recent times even people of the samurai class have come to talk openly about money.

In the mid-eighteenth century, the utilitarian ideas of the merchant class received moral reinforcement from a new school of thought called *shingaku* (studies in the human heart), a pragmatic philosophy incorporating various teachings of Confucianism, Buddhism, Taoism, and

Shintoism. In studying the human heart, shingaku scholars focused on its brighter side and recognized in every person a capacity to do moral good in all kinds of human activities. Selling merchandise of high quality, for instance, was thought to promote mutual trust among men and thereby contribute to the ethical well-being of the state. Shingaku rapidly gained popularity among the people of the merchant class, not only because its doctrines provided a moral justification for their work but also because its teachings were easy to understand and immediately applicable to their daily lives. Its teachers were well-trained, skillful speakers who were able to entertain their audience by telling instructive yet amusing stories. One such story, *Shingaku hayazomegusa* (Shingaku Dyeweed), written by Santō Kyōden (1761–1816) and published in 1790, became one of the greatest bestsellers of the eighteenth century, with sales of more than seven thousand copies. The idea that literature combines pleasure with instruction had existed in Japan since ancient times, but at no time was it so widely accepted as in the late eighteenth century.

The general outlook on life that emerges from premodern senryu has a good deal in common with the notion of the world implied in shingaku books and other popular literature of the time. A number of senryu, indeed, read like practical maxims given by wise men of the world. On the other hand, there are some senryu that look straight at the darker side of human nature. Whereas shingaku and Confucian philosophers alike concerned themselves primarily with the moral nature of man, senryu writers' area of interest occasionally seems to have extended to deeper human instincts that are egocentric, libidinous, and unruly. Sometimes they advocate harnessing those instincts but, more often than not, all they do is warn about their presence in the inmost depths of the human heart. Senryu shows its readers what real life is like, what true human nature is like. How to deal with that reality is often left to the readers.

when a man
comes asking for a loan
how honest he looks!

the game of chess:
he loses two matches, before
asking for a loan

kari ni kita toki wa shōjiki sō na kao (K 4)

shōgi wo ba niban makete wa kane wo kari (Y 12)

now that he's gone
a hot debate on the price
of a gift he brought

weeping, their eyes
glance over the mementos
to be given out[1]

[1] It was a custom that when someone died, friends and relatives gathered to share mementos of the deceased.

deta ato de moratta mono no ne no hyōgi (Y 126)

nakinagara manako wo kubaru katamiwake (Y 13)

weeping and weeping
he chooses the best
of the mementos

"He's not dead yet!"
weeping a little too early
she gets scolded

naki naki mo yoi hō wo toru katamiwake (Y 17)

mada shini mo senu no ni naite shikarareru (Y 5)

"All women . . ."
he begins, and then
glances around[1]

inch by inch
the widow's hair grows, till
it's all in a tangle[2]

[1] See the Introduction for commentary.
[2] To pledge their unchanging chastity, many women cut their hair and became lay nuns when their husbands died. It was not easy, however, for some young widows to maintain the pledge for long.

subete onna to iu mono to sokora wo mi (Y 9)

ichibu nobi nibu nobi goke no midaregami (YS 2)

"You're in the prime
of widowhood"—what a way
to compliment a woman!

visit to a new house—
on the way back, there's always
something bad to talk of

gokezakari da to homeyō mo arō no ni (YS 2)

shintaku no kaeri ni dokozo waruku ii (Y 20)

"Keep it to yourself"
he says—to how many people
nobody knows

"Don't let this worry you"
he says, then tells you something
that has to worry you

koko kiri no hanashi to yatara fure chirashi (Y 49)

ki ni wa kakerareru na to kakeru koto wo ii (Y 24)

whatever he says
is discounted fifty percent
by anyone who listens

long walk to the graveyard—
the mourners trudge on, speaking ill
of the deceased

kiku hito mo kokoro de gowari hiite oki (YS 9)

tōi tera mōja wo soshiri soshiri kuru (Y 22)

as he walks out
in anger, his umbrella
opens too wide

urgent business—
he comes rushing out
with the entire drawer

hara tatte deru karakasa wa hiraki sugi (YS 10)

hikidashi wo hinnuite kuru kyū na yō (Y 6)

learning and a ladder—
you can climb neither
if you skip a step

"Bad for my health"—
when you begin to feel so
you've begun to age

gakumon to hashigo wa tonde noborarezu (YS 10)

doku to ki no tsuita ga toshi no yori hajime (Y 64)

when it reaches
the ceiling, a man's shadow
begins to bend

a popular song:
when you learn it by heart
it's popular no more

tenjō e tsukaete magaru kagebōshi (Y 22)

hayariuta oboeru koro ni mō sutari (Y 151)

a group of travelers:
one who got the biggest send-off
is the first to poop[1]

after parting
with Mount Fuji, how rough
the road has become!

[1] While few pay attention to a seasoned traveler taking to the road, a person who rarely goes on a journey gets a big send-off.

tabidachi wa hade na ga hayaku kutabireru (Y 5)

Fuji ni wakarete kara tabi ni hone ga ore (Y 19)

when dining at an inn
"Just a little more, please"
does produce a little[1]

the Great Buddha—
marveled at by everyone
and worshiped by no one[2]

[1] "Just a little more, please" was a stock phrase a guest used when asking for a second helping of rice at a family dinner. The guest would of course receive a full bowl of rice on such an occasion.
[2] There are two immense statues of Buddha, one in Nara and the other in Kamakura. Edo townsmen were more familiar with the latter.

hatagoya wa chitto to ieba chitto nari (Y 24)

daibutsu wa miru mono ni shite tōtomazu (YS 3)

NO TRESPASSING—
thanks to the sign, you find
a shortcut

judging by the pictures
Hell looks like a more
exciting place

tōrinuke muyō de tōrinuke ga shire (YS 10)

e de mite wa jigoku no hō ga omoshiroshi (Y 71)

in Paradise
how cheap they must be—
lotus roots!¹

always for rent
the house between a machine shop
and a flour mill

¹ Lotuses were believed to be blooming in the pond of Paradise. Lotus roots are cooked
and eaten in Japan.

gokuraku wa sazo renkon ga yasukarō (Y 86)

akidana no sayū kajiya ni konaya nari (YS 10)

waiting
for another sneeze to come—
instant clownface!

the man who doesn't drink
now and then asks the barmaid
what time it is[1]

[1] The man is at a bar with his friends. In a group-oriented society like Japan, it is hard to get excused from a group activity.

ato no kusame wo matte iru baka na tsura (Y 88)

nomanu kyaku chotcho to shaku ni toki wo kiki (Y 2)

a few minutes late —
he has nothing to eat
but leeks[1]

"Looks are not
what I seek in a girl"
says a liar

[1] The scene is a sukiyaki party, probably with the meat of a duck or a wild boar as the
main ingredient. Leeks are always used in sukiyaki.

negi bakari kū mo hitoashi chigai nari (YS 9)

kiryō ni wa nozomi naki to no uso bakari (Mutamagawa 14)

the grumbler
finally stands up to leave
then grumbles for an hour

public restroom:
that's where you encounter
someone you'd rather not

guchibanashi okutte dete mo kohandoki (Y 2)

shōbenjo menboku mo nai hito ni ai (Y 18)

first one to notice
the groom's queer habit:
his sister-in-law

a modest maiden
forced to take off her clothes
by one little ant

muko no kuse imoto ga saki e mitsuke dashi (Y 2)

ari hitotsu musume zakari wo hadaka ni shi (Y 2)

a late riser—
to wake him up, you shout
"It's noon already!"

close by the man
who's hanged himself, a torn
lottery ticket

asane suru hito wo okosu wa hiru to iu (Y 7)

tomifuda no hikisaite aru kubikukuri (Y 7)

come tomorrow
waterbirds will eat whatever
comes tomorrow

from one bathtub
to another bathtub
it's all a dream[1]

[1] A man would be bathed by a midwife when he was born and by his kin when he died.

mizutori no asu kū mono wa asu nagare (SHM: An'ei 2)

tarai kara tarai ni kawaru yume no uchi (SHM: Hōreki 7)

Sources

The abbreviations used in the Japanese transliteration for indicating the original source materials are as follows:

H	*Hakoyanagi*
K	*Kawazoiyanagi*
S	*Suetsumuhana*
SHM	*Senryû hyō mankuawase*
Y	*Yanagidaru*
YS	*Yanagidaru shūi*

These collections of senryu, as well as three other books cited in this anthology (*Mutamagawa, Yanagikori*, and *Yanaibako*), are briefly described below:

Hakoyanagi. A collection of senryu published in 1785 by a poets' group headquartered in the Kōjimachi district of Edo. Reprinted in Chiba Osamu, ed., *Shodai Senryū senku shū*.

Kawazoiyanagi. Five volumes of senryu published between 1780 and 1783 by a group of poets living in the Ushigome district of Edo. Reprinted in Chiba.

Mutamagawa (complete title: *Haikai mutamagawa*). Eighteen volumes of haikai verses published in Edo between 1750 and 1776. Displaying the taste and style typical of Edo poets, these verses had a great deal of influence on senryu writers and might be said to show a state of transition from haikai to senryu. Reprinted in Yamazawa Hideo, ed., *Haikai mutamagawa*.

Senryū hyō mankuawase. Printed announcements of winning verses in Karai Senryū's maekuzuke contests held from 1757 to 1789. They differ in length, as the number of winning verses

differed in each contest. Lacking serial numbers, these announcements are customarily identified by the dates of the
contests. In this book, "SHM: Hōreki 9," for example, means
that the senryu so identified was a winning verse in one of
Senryū's contests held during the ninth year of Hōreki,
which started on January 29, 1759. *Senryū hyō mankuawase*
has not been published commercially in modern times. Although a study group named Kosenryū Kenkyūkai distributed one hundred mimeographed copies of it between 1949
and 1954, it is not easily accessible today.

Suetsumuhana (complete title: *Haifū suetsumuhana*). Four volumes of erotic senryu selected largely from *Senryū hyō mankuawase* and published between 1776 and 1801. Reprinted in
Okada Hajime, ed., *Teihon haifū suetsumuhana*.

Yanagidaru (complete title: *Haifū yanagidaru*), 167 volumes. As
explained in the Introduction, this is a series of collected
senryu published almost every year from 1765 through 1838.
The verses in the first 24 volumes were selected from *Senryū hyō mankuawase*. Okada Hajime, ed., *Haifū yanagidaru
zenshū*, is a complete modern reprint in 12 volumes.

Yanagidaru shūi (complete title: *Haifū yanagidaru shūi*). Ten volumes of senryu selected from the winning verses of maekuzuke contests refereed by Senryū and other tenja of his
time. The original edition was published in 1796–97 under
the title *Kokin maekushū*. Reprinted in Yamazawa Hideo,
ed., *Haifū yanagidaru shūi*.

Yanagikori. Three volumes of senryu published probably between
1784 and 1786. The poets who wrote them lived in the Kōjimachi district of Edo but belonged to a group different
from the one that produced *Hakoyanagi*. Only volume 3
has survived. Reprinted in Chiba.

Yanaibako. Four volumes of senryu written by a group of poets living in the Azabu district of Edo and published between 1783
and 1786. Volume 3 is missing. The extant volumes are reprinted in Chiba.

Selected Bibliography

Works in English

Bito, Sanryu, comp. *Senryū: Haiku Reflections of the Times*. Atlanta: Mangajin, 1997.

Blyth, R. H. *Edo Satirical Verse Anthologies*. Tokyo: Hokuseido, 1961.

——. *Japanese Life and Character in Senryu*. Tokyo: Hokuseido, 1960.

——. *Oriental Humour*. Tokyo: Hokuseido, 1959.

——. *Senryu: Japanese Satirical Verses*. Tokyo: Hokuseido, 1949.

Bownas, Geoffrey and Anthony Thwaite, trans. "Sixty Senryu." In their *Penguin Book of Japanese Verse*. Baltimore: Penguin, 1964.

Brown, J. C. *Senryu: Poems of the People*. Rutland, Vt.: Tuttle, 1991.

Higginson, William J. "Beyond Haiku." In his *The Haiku Handbook*. New York: McGraw-Hill, 1985.

Hodgson, James D. "Senryu Through the Ages." In his *American Senryu*. Tokyo: The Japan Times, 1992.

Isaacson, Harold J., ed. *The Throat of the Peacock: A Book of Modern Senryu on Parents and Children*. New York: Theatre Art Books, 1977.

Keene, Donald. "Waka Poetry: Comic Poetry." In his *World Within Walls*. New York: Grove, 1976.

Levy, Howard S. and Ohsawa Junko, trans. *One Hundred Senryu*. South Pasadena, Calif.: Langstaff, 1979.

Solt, John. "Willow Leaftips." In Sumie Jones, ed., *Imaging/Reading Eros*. Bloomington, Ind.: East Asian Studies Center, Indiana University, 1996.

Watson, Burton, trans. "Forty-Seven Senryu." In Hiroaki Sato and Burton Watson, eds., *From the Country of Eight Islands*. New York: Anchor Books, 1981.

Works in Japanese

All publishers below are located in Tokyo.

Adachi, Yoshio. *Edo senryū no shiteki kenkyū*. Kazama Shobō, 1967.

——. *Kanshō Edo senryū*. Chōbunsha, 1968.

Asō, Isoji. *Warai no kenkyū*. Tōkyōdō, 1947.

Bitō, Sanryū. *Senryū nyūmon*. Yūzankaku, 1989.

Chiba, Osamu, ed. *Shodai Senryū senku shū*. 2 vols. Iwanami Shoten, 1995.

Hamada, Giichirō, ed. *Edo senryū jiten*. Tōkyōdō, 1968.

Hamada, Giichirō and Morikawa Akira, eds. *Senryū, kyōka*. Kadokawa Shoten, 1977.

Hamada, Giichirō et al., eds. *Haifū yanagidaru*. 10 vols. Shakai Shisōsha, 1985–88.

Iwata, Kurō. *Edo senryū wo yomu*. Yūseidō, 1991.

Kanda, Bōjin. *Edo senryū wo tanoshimu*. Asahi Shinbunsha, 1989.

Kasuya, Hiroki. *Shinpen senryū daijiten*. Tōkyōdō, 1995.

Kosenryū Kenkyūkai, ed. *Senryū hyō mankuawase*. Kosenryū Kenkyūkai, 1949–54.

Kusumoto, Kenkichi and Yamamura Yū. *Shin senryū e no shōtai*. Nichibō Shuppansha, 1980.

Miyata, Masanobu, ed. *Haifū yanagidaru*. Shinchōsha, 1984.

Okada, Hajime, ed. *Haifū yanagidaru zenshū*. 12 vols. Sanseidō, 1976–78.

——. *Teihon haifū suetsumuhana*. Yūkō Shobō, 1969.

Okitsu, Kaname. *Tanbō Edo senryū*. Jiji Tsūshinsha, 1990.

Saitō, Daiyū. *Gendai senryū nyūmon*. Taimatsusha, 1979.

Senryū Nenkan Kankō Iinkai, ed. *Senryū nenkan*. 1997 edition. Shizensha, 1997.

Shimoyama, Hiroshi. *Edo kosenryū no sekai*. Kōdansha, 1994.

Sugimoto, Nagashige, ed. "Senryū shū." In *Nihon koten bungaku taikei* 57. Iwanami Shoten, 1958.

Suzuki, Katsutada. *Karai Senryū*. Shintensha, 1982.

Suzuki, Katsutada, ed. "Senryū." In *Nihon koten bungaku zenshū* 46. Shōgakukan, 1971.

Tanabe, Teinosuke. *Kosenryū fūzoku jiten*. Seiabō, 1962.

Tokizane, Shinko. *Yūfuren*. Kadokawa Shoten, 1996.

Tokizane, Shinko, ed. *Senryū*. Sakuhinsha, 1995.

Yamafuji, Shōji, Bitō Sanryū, and Daiichi Seimei, eds. *Heisei sarariiman senryū kessaku sen: dai rokkan*. Kōdansha, 1996.

Yamaji, Kanko. *Kosenryū meiku sen*. Chikuma Shobō, 1968.

Yamazawa, Hideo, ed. *Haifū yanagidaru*. 4 vols. Iwanami Shoten, 1995.

——. *Haifū yanagidaru shūi*. 2 vols. Iwanami Shoten, 1995.

——. *Haikai mutamagawa*. 4 vols. Iwanami Shoten, 1984–85.

Yamazawa, Hideo and Kasuya Hiroki, eds. *Yanagidaru meiku sen*. 2 vols. Iwanami Shoten, 1995.

Yomiuri Shinbunsha, ed. *Jiji senryū hyakunen*. Yomiuri Shinbunsha, 1990.

Yoshida, Seiichi. "Senryū shū." In *Koten Nihon bungaku zenshū* 33. Chikuma Shobō, 1961.